SS Panzer Battalion 501

SS Panzer Battalion 501

Tigers in the Ardennes

Hugues Wenkin and Christian Dujardin

Pen & Sword
MILITARY

First published in Great Britain in 2023 and in this format in 2025 by
Pen & Sword Military
An imprint of Pen & Sword Books Limited
Yorkshire – Philadelphia

ISBN 978 1 39905 617 5

A CIP catalogue record for this book is available from the British Library

Typeset by Mac Style
Printed in the UK by CPI Group (UK) Ltd, Croydon, CR0 4YY.

The Publisher's authorised representative in the EU for product safety is Authorised Rep Compliance Ltd., Ground Floor, 71 Lower Baggot Street, Dublin D02 P593, Ireland.

www.arccompliance.com

For a complete list of Pen & Sword titles please contact

PEN & SWORD BOOKS LIMITED
47 Church Street, Barnsley, South Yorkshire, S70 2AS, England
E-mail: enquiries@pen-and-sword.co.uk
Website: www.pen-and-sword.co.uk
or
PEN AND SWORD BOOKS
1950 Lawrence Rd, Havertown, PA 19083, USA
E-mail: Uspen-and-sword@casematepublishers.com
Website: www.penandswordbooks.com

FSC www.fsc.org
MIX
Paper | Supporting responsible forestry
FSC® C013604

Contents

Introduction

The Battle of the Bulge was the last major German attempt to alter the inexorable course of the war on the Western Front. Operationally, the aim of the offensive was to cut off the American armies in the south from their Commonwealth allies in the north by launching an armoured spike to the port of Antwerp. The idea of Adolf Hitler, who was behind the '*Wacht am Rhein*' operation, was to create a trap in Holland in order to provoke a second Dunkirk for the British. Politically, the Führer hoped that the impact of such a defeat would force the British, and indeed the Western Allies as a whole, to negotiate a separate peace with the Reich; such a turnaround would then allow Berlin to regroup the Wehrmacht in the East in order to stop the Soviet armies from sweeping into Poland. At the tip of the German system, to the north of the Ardennes offensive, was Gepanzerte Kampfgruppe Peiper. It was on the shoulders of its commander, SS Obersturmbannführer Joachim Peiper, at dawn on 16 December 1944, that German hopes would rest. The verdict was decided a long time ago: the operation had proved to be a bitter failure. The reasons for the German defeat were numerous, touching as much on strategy and the configuration of the forces present as they did on logistical aspects.

Hitler outlines his plan for his last-chance offensive to von Rundsted's staff. (*BWM*)

The fighting was characterized by the engagement of two units equipped with Panzer VI Ausf. B, the famous Tiger IIs, which the GIs nicknamed 'King Tiger'. One of them made a lasting impression: the schwere SS-Panzer-Abteilung 501. Placed in the wake of Kampfgruppe Peiper, some of its elements were caught in the La Gleize trap with the SS Obersturmbannführer's other vehicles. After the battle, eleven of the twelve Tiger IIs engaged were found abandoned in an area reaching from Stavelot to La Gleize: a casualty rate of

The crew of the M10 who destroyed Tiger 222 pose in front of their machine. (*NARA*)

almost 100 percent for a vehicle considered to be one of the most powerful fighting weapons of the Second World War!

The ratio is, to say the least, surprising. Indeed, with its 180 mm frontal armour on the turret and 150 mm on the hull, together with the powerful 88 mm barrel, it did not seem to fear any of its contemporary adversaries. However, the fact is that in the Ardennes, while it was served by exceptional crews, including several aces, and often benefitted from the element of surprise, it still suffered a bitter failure.

The story of this heavy tank battalion with its impressive record of 1,000 destroyed vehicles is therefore something of a myth. This very powerful unit, which was destined to be the spearhead of the German army, failed miserably on a hill in the Belgian Ardennes. An analysis of the causes of the breakdowns, destructions and abandonments makes it possible to better apprehend the real effectiveness of these heavy tanks in this theatre of operations, as well as to explain the origins of the high attrition rate affecting these mastodons of almost 70 tonnes.

After meticulous study, the odyssey of the great beasts of the 501 can now be reconstructed point by point. It took patience, critical thinking and insight to solve the enigma and understand the causes of this tactical failure. How many false leads have been unexplored? The traps for the historian are indeed numerous! Only objectivity and logic

The wreckage of Tiger 222 after being cut up by the scrap merchants. This was all that remained of the spearhead of the German offensive. (*Jacobs Bibliothèque de Stavelot*)

can foil them. Combat reports and testimonies have been sifted through and compared. As is often the case, accounts diverge, and it was necessary to call upon the most intangible elements: period photographs and numerous visits to the locations themselves. In the manner of a judicial reconstruction, the testimonies are dissected according to the configuration of the place. Surprising as it may seem, many places have remained as they were seventy years earlier. The land does not lie! The terrain does not forget! It keeps the stigma of the battle and guides the researcher in his quest for the truth. The result gives a clear picture of what the chaos of battle was like. After the investigation, conclusions must be drawn to understand the root causes of the failure.

This study therefore has the double objective of reconstructing the facts and explaining why, in the end, no other result was possible. Part of this text appeared in a previous book, *The Fate of the Peiper Tiger* (original title: *Stavelot La Gleize, le destin des tigers de Peiper*), which is now out of print. Some of the information it contained is republished here. Our research continues and we are constantly discovering new information. This has enabled us to clarify certain events and to go into greater depth in the evocation of the destiny of these mythical chariots. For those readers who own the original book, they will discover many new additions here. Four more lost tanks have been identified, making this the most accurate book ever written on the subject. We will not limit ourselves here to simply mention what happened in the Stavelot–La Gleize sector, as our research has led us as far as Bastogne, where two Tiger tanks were also lost by the schwere SS-Panzer-Abteilung 501. As you may have noticed, this is a first volume. A second volume is in preparation, which will deal with the fate of 1. SS-Panzer-Regiment in the Battle of the Bulge.

Chapter 1

The Station of the Cross of KG Peiper

Order of Battle

The Gepanzerte Kampfgruppe was led by Obersturmbannführer Joachim Peiper. Very powerful, the formation was at the cutting edge of the German military machine and formed the spearhead of 1. SS-Panzer-Division 'Leibstandarte Adolf Hitler', under the command of SS-Oberführer Wilhelm Mohnke. It was headed by I. SS-Panzer-Korps, which was an integral part of 6. Panzer-Armee.[1]

Peiper's Kampfgruppe (KG) was a mixed armoured force, as it was not possible to assemble enough Panther and Panzer IVs to form a Panzer Regiment according to official manning tables. In practice, there should have been four Panther Kompanie in the first Abteilung and four Panzer IV companies in the second. In this instance, it was only materially possible to form two Kompanie of each. Therefore, half of the Peiper battleship element was composed of conventional elements to form the equivalent of a tank battalion. The contingency detachment consisted of two Kompanie of Panther

Sepp Dietrich commanded the 6. Panzer-Armee, which was to attack Antwerp at full speed. (*NARA*)

Peiper's Panzerspitze had Panzergrenadiers with Sdk Fz 251 Ausf.Ds. (*NARA*)

I. SS Pz-Rgt 1 was equipped with Panthers. These were photographed the day before the battle. (*Rights reserved*)

The 6. and 7. Kompagnie of I. SS-Pz-Rgt 1 were equipped with Panzer IV Ausf. Hs. This one belonged to the Leibstandarte and was photographed in Italy. (*NARA*)

Ausf. G and two of Panzer IV Ausf. H. These came from Abteilungen I and II of SS-Panzer-Regiment 1, which is why there were Panzer-Kompanie 1, 2, 6 and 7 in the unit. These units were supervised by the Stab of I. Abteilung of SS-Sturmbannführer Werner Poetschke. The schwere SS-Panzer-Abteilung 501, a Tiger tank battalion under the command of SS-Obersturmbannführer Heinz von Westernhagen, completed the strength of the armoured regiment, which should normally have had two Abteilungen.[2]

The unit was supported by:

- The Panzergrenadiere of III. (gep)/SS-Panzergrenadier-Regiment 2
- Self-propelled 150mm Sd.Kfz. 138/1 of 13(IG)/SS-Panzergrenadier-Regiment 2
- The paratroopers of 9. Fallschirmjäger-Regiment, under the command of Oberst von Hoffmann
- Flak-Sturm-Abteilung 84 (Sf.) under Major von Sacken
- Flakpanzer IV Wirbelwind of 10. (flak)/SS-Panzer-Regiment 1
- The sappers of 3. (gep)/SS-Panzer-Pionier-Battalion 1

Peiper therefore had a completely autonomous unit. Most were elite troops equipped with heavy, modern and efficient equipment, although the KG only received the equivalent of three full tanks out of the five promised. When considering a Tiger II only had a range of 170 km, this was not necessarily enough to launch itself at the forefront of an offensive of such a scale as that in the Ardennes.

Mission Impossible?

The objective assigned to Peiper was to secure the crossing point over the Meuse at Ombret-Rausa, near Huy. The breakthrough had to be quick and decisive in order to maintain the element of surprise, the main weapon behind the successful Blitzkrieg of May 1940. Peiper was ordered to achieve this result within 24 hours of the start of the offensive. His axis of attack passed through Losheim, Poteau, Ligneuville, Stavelot, Trois-Ponts, Werbomont and Ouffet. Von der Heydte's paratroopers and Skorzeny's commandos were responsible for providing support by disrupting the enemy's rear. Times, however, had changed. Four years had passed since the Sedan breakthrough. The Allies now had control of the air, reinforced anti-tank resources and impeccable logistical support, surpassing the Third Reich in all respects. Although the KG had superior weaponry and the element of surprise, these were its only advantages. Peiper's mission can therefore be described as difficult and risky. It was a race against time, and every minute lost would reduce the Germans' chances of success.

A Difficult Start

The beginning of the attack on Peiper was characterised by a series of misunderstandings that caused delays in the schedule. First of all, there was the resistance of the 99th Infantry

The bridges over the Meuse were targeted by KG Peiper. (*NARA*)

Division, which the men of 12. Volksgrenadier-Division only managed to push through late in the day. Although the American front was broken, the SS were still delayed: the bridge between Hallschlag and Losheim having been destroyed in September. This forced the KG to make detours that were costly in time and fuel. At the exit of Losheim, another bridge was also out of order and Peiper was forced to turn west and fall back into the lines held by 3. Fallschirmjäger-Division at Lanzerath, around midnight.[3] The latter were trampling in front of a minefield set up in front of Bucholz. With the help of his tanks, the SS-Obersturmbannführer allowed the paratroopers to take the position. On his way, he also took Honsfeld, where he captured 130 vehicles and 15 US anti-tank guns.

K. Wortmann was part of a Flak unit, riding Wirbelwinds: quadruple flak guns mounted on a turret on a Panzer IV chassis. Wortmann recounted the battle on 17 December, which took place in the locality of Honsfeld:

> *Four of our tanks were leading the column. Our battery commander and platoon leader were in the first two vehicles. Because of the narrow bends at the entrance to the village, we had to drive slowly and could hardly see anything. Suddenly we heard the sound of an explosion. Our first tank was hit. It drove a few more metres and then suddenly stopped. Immediately afterwards, the second tank was eliminated. By chance I saw the direction from*

GIs from the 99th Infantry Division. Although inexperienced, the right wing of this division would withstand the initial attack for several hours. (*NARA*)

which the shot came and I opened fire in the same direction, which silenced the American guns. Now we could continue. In the middle of the village, the firing resumed. Our 3rd Engineer Company was fired upon from the windows and skylights of the neighbouring houses. We responded to the shooting and soon afterwards the Americans came out of their hiding places with their hands raised. There were many dead and wounded on both sides. We had to leave our company commander, Vögler, Hauptscharführer Schröder and the entire crew of the first two tanks of the anti-aircraft artillery.[4]

The Wirbelwind was a Panzer IV on which a quadruple 20-mm anti-aircraft turret had been mounted.(*NARA*)

The massacre of eighty-six GIs who were taken prisoner at Baugnez would forever tarnish Joachim Peiper's reputation. (*NARA*)

The capture of Honsfeld opened the road to Schoppen, but the road proved to be impassable to a quick passage of vehicles. Instead, Peiper decided to make another diversion via Bullange, where he seized 227,000 litres of fuel that US prisoners had to empty into his tanks.[5] Peiper was delighted with this capture, as the diversion to bypass Losheim had severely depleted his meagre reserves of the precious liquid. It was only at 1030hrs that the invasion column resumed its route towards Schoppen, without worrying about the fire from the 612th Tank Destroyer Battalion. Most of the American soldiers taken prisoner were initially guarded, but were later massacred. The most infamous exaction of the Peiper column took place at Baugnez, where eighty-six GIs were shot. The SS left Ligneuville and ran into the rear of Combat Command B of the 9th Armored Division.

On the evening of 17 December, the general alert was given on the American front. After a period of hesitation due to the initial surprise, the US officers reacted effectively. The valleys of the Belgian Ardennes were steep, and river crossings were only possible at bridges where the banks were developed. The GIs therefore organised their defence based on the destruction of the bridges. These were modest in size, but the autumn rains had increased the amount of water in the rivers. Moreover, their steep banks were impossible

The GIs thought they would be able to rest in the Ardennes, but the alarm was quickly raised. These soldiers are receiving coffee and donuts from the US Red Cross. (*NARA*)

to traverse without levelling them first. Consequently, whoever held the bridges would hold the Ardennes. In Stavelot, a small medieval town nestled in a meander of the River Amblève, the 291st Combat Engineer Battalion was in charge of its defence. The unit was completely unable to hold the town on its own, but some men went up to meet the Germans on the Ligneuville road to set up an anti-tank blockade. Thirteen mines were placed on the road and the men took up their positions with a bazooka. The location was judiciously chosen to be favourable for defence. Indeed, at this place the road formed a ledge on the sides of a steep rocky slope, and the US pioneers managed to block a German reconnaissance unit.[6] It was now late and night was falling, so Peiper decided to reorganise his column, which had been disrupted by the day's many setbacks.

Questioned on 7 September 1945, while he was a prisoner of war, the Obersturmbannführer gave the following testimony to Major Kenneth W. Heckler:

> *On 17 December, at about 1600hrs, my tanks reached Stavelot, which was strongly defended. We still tried to enter the town during the night, but the terrain caused us many problems. We could only reach Stavelot by the main road. It was bordered by rocks on the*

> *left and a deep gorge on the right. For this reason, I ordered the 6th and 7th companies to attack Trois-Ponts via Wanne. At about 1800hrs my men were again attacked by American infantrymen hidden behind a hill about 800 metres south of Stavelot. When the counter-attack was repulsed, I used more armoured infantry and approached the outskirts of the town. After very strong resistance, I had to interrupt the attack and decided to wait for infantry reinforcements.*[7]

By this prudent decision, Peiper lost twelve hours that evening! The Americans took the opportunity to reinforce Stavelot with the 526th Armored Infantry Battalion, including a company of 3-inch anti-tank guns and several tank fighters of the 825th Tank Destroyer Battalion. The position was strategically useful for the US command because on the

The Stavelot bridge photographed after the battle. The first bridge on the right bank of the Amblève was summarily repaired, after being blown up in the evening of 19 December. (*Jacobs Bibliothèque de Stavelot*)

town's high ground, on a place called "la haute levée", was a huge fuel depot that must not, under any circumstances, fall in the wrong hands …[8]

Although the American front was broken through on 16 December, the exploitation of the surprise attack was made impossible the next day by the severe loss of time. On top of this, the detours cost Joachim Peiper a great deal of fuel.

The Flight to Safety

On 18 December, after wasting these precious hours, Peiper finally went on the attack. The American engineers were not yet able to destroy the Stavelot bridge and at around 1000hrs the Germans succeeded in driving the US troops out of the town. They took

The N33 road between Stavelot and Trois-Ponts was used by KG Peiper. At that time it was still a dirt road. (*Jacobs Bibliothèque de Stavelot*)

The American Thunderbolts caused major losses in the column. (*NARA*)

the N33 towards Trois-Ponts: a necessary passage to reach Huy. Meanwhile, the SS had to cross the Amblève, the meandering river which once again stood in the way of the Obersturmbannführer's troops. Here C Company of the 51st Combat Engineer Battalion had plenty of time to prepare the town's defences, and the bridge was blown up in front of the SS. Another river, the Salm, also flows through the town, but the bridge over it vanished in front of the SS detachment, who had been sent the day before via Wanne. Peiper now had to find another crossing point on the Amblève.

The next bridge was at Cheneux. It was crossed quickly, but at its exit the Thunderbolts of the 9th Tactical Air Force bombed the column. A Panther G was destroyed, a Kubelwagen was blown up, including the officers occupying it, and two immobilized Sd Kfz 251s blocked the bridge. After having recovered their composure, the SS rushed on Neufmoulin to cross the next river: the Lienne. Peiper also launched a reconnaissance mission on the other side of the river via a wooden footbridge at Rahier, the aim of this mission being to take the bridge from behind. This small bridge was impassable for heavy tanks, and, once again, the main bridge at Neufmoulin was blown up in front of the invading column.[9] The reconnaissance unit, already across the river, advanced towards Werbomont, where it encountered an anti-tank position of the 117th Infantry Regiment, 30th Infantry Division. As the day progressed, Peiper decided to entrench at

Peiper's advance was stopped at Stoumont station. One of the disabled Panthers here was equipped with Stahlrollen (special steel-rimmed wheels). (*NARA*)

La Gleize. This small village occupied a strategic position on the plateau overlooking the Cheneux bridge, where he left a detachment to maintain his bridgehead on the left bank of the Amblève.

The outcome of the day was mixed for the Germans: they had managed to cross the valley of the Amblève, but the road to Huy was still cut off as the bridge over the Lienne was destroyed. The next day, Peiper's men had to go deeper into the valley to reach the next bridge and re-cross the Amblève at a point where the Lienne was no longer an obstacle. The objective on 19 December would be a ford located at Targnon on the N33 road.

The Stoppage

The 119th Infantry Regiment, reinforced by ten Shermans commanded by Major Macht, took up position in Stoumont,[10] located after La Gleize on the ford road. The St Edouard preventorium, an imposing building with thick walls, provided shelter for 250 civilians, most of them children. The civilians were relegated to the cellars while the US

A reconnaissance M5A1 followed by a Sherman M4 (75), 743rd Tank Battalion, on their way to the front to counter Peiper. (*NARA*)

infantry took up positions at the windows. Peiper launched the 2nd Panther company, followed by the 3rd Paras battalion integrated into his column. The Americans retreated, leaving 267 prisoners, while the SS only lost one Panther. To ensure the protection of his right flank, the Obersturmbannführer launched two reconnaissance missions. One from La Gleize, the other from Stoumont, but both were quickly stopped by anti-aircraft gun fire. If the reconnaissance had been more enterprising, they would have discovered a huge fuel depot behind a thin curtain of defence that the Americans were in the process of evacuating.[11] The gods of war were definitely in the Allies' favour.

Colonel Sutherland, commander of 119th IR, reacted calmly to the fall of Stoumont and the rout of his III/119th IR. He set up a powerful roadblock 1 kilometre from his headquarters and ordered his 1st Battalion to take up position in a steep and heavily wooded area. Two 90-mm anti-aircraft guns, placed in anti-tank mode, provided reinforcements, one belonging to the 143rd AAA, the other to the 110th AAA.[12] An M10 Tank Destroyer, the A-2[13] of 823rd TDB, was on the defensive,[14] as well as the Shermans of 743rd TB. The second 90-mm gun of the 110th AAA was positioned 500 metres back, just in front of the Lorcé halt, level with a wood depot.

The 90-mm anti-aircraft gun was often used during the Battle of the Bulge in anti-tank missions. (*NARA*)

Although the German attack slowed down at around 1200hrs, it soon resumed in earnest. The Sherman C-10[15] had the thankless task of slowing down the enemy charge and was in the frontline at the roadblock. On the German side, five Panthers were still intact and continued to push forward with the Panzergrenadier of 11th Company, SS-Panzergrenadier Regiment 2 (11./ SS-Pz.Gren.Rgt. 2) accompanied by Fallschirmjäger.[16] While the infantry tried to bypass the roadblock through the forest, the Panther 215 of Unterscharführer[17] Krüger drove at the head of the pack. Fifty metres before the last bend in the road leading to the new frontline, the leading Panther entered the line of fire of the Sherman C-10, which fired and disabled Krüger's tank. The Panther 215 remained immobilised on the left-hand side of the road, but did not catch fire. The killing of the beast was recorded in the 119th IR's diary at 1300hrs. The driver of the 215, Oskar Guttmann, was wounded and transported to the field hospital based at Froidcour castle.

The Taking of Cheneux

The weather continued to favour the Allies, who took advantage of the respite caused by their tactical victory at Stoumont to reinforce their position around the invasion column. The 82nd Airborne Division arrived in extremis at Werbomont. The first thing to be done, in the eyes of its leader, Major General James Gavin, was to ensure the deployment of his division to a safe position. He set his sights on the left bank of the Amblève, but to do this he had to clear the German bridgehead at Cheneux. From there, the SS were

Paratroopers of the 504th PIR, 82nd Airborne Division, move towards Cheneux. (*NARA*)

An Sd Kfz 10 (1 tonne) anti-aircraft gun destroyed in the hamlet of Cheneux. (*NARA*)

able to take the American positions along the banks of the river in reverse. Colonel Reuben Tucker's 504th PIR was given the difficult task, and its success was the key to the security of the defensive line. The II/504th PIR received the order to take Rahier. The paratroopers set off at about 1900hrs on 19 December and after a long six-hour march through the steep valley of the Lienne, they arrived at their objective to find it empty of enemies. Quickly, the 'All Americans' secured their hold with the help of C Coy, 307th Engineer Combat Battalion. The civilians questioned informed the Americans that there was a very high concentration of enemy troops in the area, although the figures they gave were exaggerated: 125 vehicles, including about 30 tanks. Colonel Tucker informed Gavin of the situation.[18] He wanted to act quickly to surprise the Germans with an infantry attack to seize their tanks and turn them against their former owners. Tucker brought with him a vital asset: a collection of Panzerfauste captured during the previous Dutch campaign.

The attack started on 20 December at 1300hrs. It was led by I/504th PIR (without its A Coy), its objective being to reduce Peiper's bridgehead at Cheneux and to retake the bridge over the Amblève. Moments before the attack, the Germans were alerted

A paratrooper from 82nd Airborne Division presses forward in the assault. Barbed wire fences would prove to be a hindrance in the Ardennes. (*NARA*)

by the encounter, 800 metres east of the town, between a US patrol and a German mounted courrier flanked by Landsers. They were followed by a company-strength column advancing on both sides of the main road towards Rahier. The affair turned into a head-on collision, and Major General Gavin witnessed the ferocity of the engagement:

> *I was there for the attack, the German firepower was impressive. They were using a lot of 20-mm anti-aircraft guns. A weapon the infantry consider the most uncomfortable to face* [sic]. *Colonel Tucker had deployed his I/504th against the Germans trying to get out of Cheneux.*[19] *It was a tough fight and when darkness fell on the battlefield, C and B companies were under tremendous fire from the village. Undeterred, Colonel Tucker ordered Lieutenant Colonel Willard E. Harrison, the battalion commander, to launch a night attack. Harrison had parachuted with me into Normandy and was a very brave soldier. They now had two Tank Destroyers,*[20] *which made them feel about the same strength as anything they would encounter. As they pushed towards Cheneux they encountered well organised defences surrounded by barbed wire.*[21] *The opposing force turned out to be the SS-Panzergrenadier Regiment 2, heavily reinforced with mobile anti-aircraft guns, mortars, machine guns and assault artillery.*[22]

The M36 Jackson was a tank fighter with a powerful 90-mm gun. (*NARA*)

To counter this heavy fire and drive through the 400 metres of open ground, the two companies attacked in four waves about 50 metres apart. As the main American assault waves were spotted in the darkness, the SS opened up with intense and accurate fire. Twice the attackers were driven back, both times with gaping holes in their ranks. The first two waves were almost completely decimated. C Company hit the fences and, having no shears available, were momentarily pinned down. Eventually the two Tank Destroyers made their way to the front and began to target the German guns. With their support, a third assault was launched on the village, and this time a few men managed to reach the outlying houses. In a brief, close fight, the paratroopers silenced some of the anti-aircraft weapons and machine guns before setting up a defensive position to protect this small pocket until reinforcements arrived. Meanwhile, the battalion commander set up his command post in a house at the entrance to the village.[23] During the night, the situation turned into a fierce street fight, with every single house fiercely fought over. Tucker decided to manoeuvre and undertake a broad envelopment using the Third Battalion, commanded by Lieutenant Colonel Julian Cook.[24] The US attackers made a wide flanking movement over very rough terrain, which took six hours, but by the end of the day they dominated the bridge over the Amblève. The Germans were surrounded in the village and had lost their command. The affair proved costly. Tucker lost 225 dead and wounded, mainly in his two assault companies. B Company had only eighteen men left and no officers. C Company still had thirty-eight men and three officers. Few Germans were captured. The rear guard fought to the end, but most of the Cheneux garrison who were still alive escaped during the night. Tucker captured anti-aircraft vehicles and a 105-mm howitzer battery, as well as many vehicles. The performance of the 504th PIR was remarkable: the anti-aircraft spitting hellfire had been put out of action by grenades! For this feat of arms, the I/504th received a presidential citation.

General Major James Gavin commanded the 82nd Airborne Division during the fighting in 1944. (*NARA*)

In the evening of 19 December, the 504th Parachute Infantry Regiment of the 82nd Airborne Division recaptured Cheneux after fierce fighting and established a bridgehead on the German side of the Lienne. Between Stavelot and La Gleize, on the right flank of the SS, a first American point was pushed back by very precise artillery fire, and a pincer

American 81-mm mortars pound La Gleize. (*NARA*)

manoeuvre started to take shape. The hammer was also close: a battalion of mortars stood prepared to pound La Gleize.

Meanwhile, the Americans were making life difficult for the rear of the German column, trying to retake the bridge at Stavelot. Hard fighting broke out in the small town to prevent Peiper from being reinforced.

Friedrich Pfeifer, former commander of Rudi Sandig's 2nd Company of Battalion 1, recounted the fight for the bridge:

> *Without having had any direct contact with the enemy, my company, which was the spearhead of our 2nd Regiment, reached the southern part of Stavelot on the Amblève. At that time, this part of the town was not occupied by the Americans. However, we were bombarded by American artillery throughout our march on Stavelot. Just in front of the bridge was a destroyed tank of our Panzer Regiment and an arch of the bridge was blown up just before we arrived. We therefore concluded that the northern part of the town, the largest, must be in American hands. In order to lead my men to a successful attack, I needed the support of a heavy company. But my regimental commander ordered me to attack immediately, without taking into account my request. All this took place thirty minutes after our arrival from the bridge over the Amblève in the afternoon of the 19th. After placing two sections of my company on each side of the bridge as covering troops, I set off with two other sections and gained the north bank of the Amblève with*

An Sd Kfz 251/9 Ausf. D is destroyed in Stavelot square by a Sherman from B Company, 743rd Tank Battalion. (*Rights reserved*)

great difficulty, having used the destroyed arches of the bridge. Suddenly we were shelled by US artillery and had grenades thrown at us from the old abbey and the houses nearby. On the roof of the abbey were large flags with red crosses, meaning that this building was used as a hospital. We did not manage to take it. We finally gathered in the bushes by the river and defended ourselves desperately. We had no more grenades or ammunition for our machine guns. Waiting for help was out of the question: the enemy had started to fire flares since nightfall and movement was impossible. We were therefore forced to abandon the north bank of the Amblève at dawn on 20 December. Still under enemy fire, we marched through the icy water of the river to join our own troops. We lost twenty-three men in this mad and ill-prepared attack. My liaison officer, Biedenkamp, can testify to the truth of this report.[25]

The Tragic Cauldron

By 20 December, Peiper was not quite surrounded, being connected to his rear through a concrete bridge between Stavelot and Trois-Ponts at Petit Spay. Pioneers of the 2nd Battalion of the 2nd Regiment of 1. SS-Panzer-Division, managed to get through and reinforce Peiper for the last time. L70 Jagdpanzer IVs engaged the small bridge and caused it to collapse. The 3rd German Engineer Company tried twice to launch a bridgehead, but the effective intervention of the American artillery prevented it. The last

An Sd Kfz 251/21 Ausf D. found abandoned in the cauldron of La Gleize. (*NARA*)

German reinforcements took position at Cheneux, towards which the US paratroopers of 504th PIR were heading. On the evening of 21 December, the paratroopers finally recaptured the small town after some very tough hand-to-hand combat and grenade fighting.

Their colleagues of the 505th took position in Trois-Ponts, while those of the 508th were further south on the road and prevented Hansen's SS Panzers from bypassing the

A Sherman M4A3 76 (W) from 740th Tank Battalion, photographed at Remouchamp after the fighting. (*Authors' collection*)

small town. Peiper had dug in at Stoumont and La Gleize. The St Edouard preventorium became a German fortress, much to the dismay of the refugees still hiding in its cellars.

During the night of 21 December, Shermans of 740th Tank Battalion gradually reduced the German position, and although the preventorium changed hands, it was now a ruin. In the morning, the 250 civilians who had miraculously survived, but who were still haggard, were finally evacuated by US infantrymen of the 30th ID, who continued their push towards the centre of Stoumont. They were supported by Task Force *Jordan*, which attacked from the north from Spa.

On the road between Stavelot and Trois-Ponts, the pincer movement became more and more visible thanks to the intervention of Task Force *Lovelady*. This unit's mission was to cut the N33 and to link up with paratroopers from 505th PIR entrenched in Trois-Ponts. Its momentum was cut by Tiger 132 and anti-tank guns, which were still blocked on the other side of the Amblève by the collapse of the Petit Spay footbridge.

Endgame in the Northern Sector

The next morning, the failure of the Germans was confirmed. They had to evacuate Stoumont, but the road to Stavelot was definitively cut off by *Lovelady*. La Gleize had become an entrenched camp by force of circumstance. Moreover, Peiper had used up most of his precious fuel in the fighting of the previous days and so tried to parachute in petrol around 2000hrs. To mark his perimeter, he used a tight fire of tracer bullets. Despite this ingenious device, however, the Luftwaffe, decidedly inefficient, dropped most of the containers outside the perimeter.

On 23 December the SS position became a hell on earth after being hammered by US artillery. The situation was desperate and Peiper obtained the authorization to evacuate what would come to be known as the Cauldron of La Gleize from SS-Oberfuhrer Wilhelm Mohnke, the commander of his division.[26]

The Germans fled through a small gate. In the valley at the foot of the village, a footbridge remained at La Venne, which had been built to facilitate the construction of a large railway bridge. Unfortunately, the railway bridge was unusable, having been pounded by enemy artillery. However, its protective shadow extended to the small footbridge and it allowed Peiper to evacuate secretly in the early hours of 24 December. To reach the main body of 1. SS-Panzer-Division 'Leibstandarte Adolf Hitler', his men had to cross the Salm, a tributary of the Amblève. Although it had not yet snowed in this part of the Belgian Ardennes, it was already freezing cold and the torrent of icy water must have been a particularly trying ordeal for his defeated men.

Peiper's adventure at La Gleize ended with the abandonment of all his rolling stock. The losses of Stoumont and Cheneux were nothing compared to what he left behind in the cauldron. An eyewitness, Mr. Grégoire, made the count on his return to the scene:

- 47 Sdkfz 251 Ausf D of various types
- 7 Panzer IV Ausf. H
- 13 Panther Ausf. G (one with steel wheels)
- 6 Tiger II
- 6 Bison (155mm howitzer)
- 3 Sdkfz 234/2 Puma
- 1 Wirbelwind
- 14 miscellaneous vehicles[27]

A very rare Panther Ausf G. Stahlrollen found on the main road through La Gleize. (*NARA*)

The famous tank field at La Gleize, where most of Peiper's SPWs were found. (*NARA via 30th ID*)

These were all finally destroyed with explosives by US engineers to prevent the SS from trying to recover them in a possible counter-attack. The G4 report[28] of the 30th ID stated:

> *Our office received information on 24 December at 1145hrs that a unit of our division had captured 36 tanks, 70 half-tracks, 12 assault guns and 66 miscellaneous vehicles. As the Divisional Ordnance did not have equipment large enough to evacuate the heavy equipment, Lieutenant Colonel Frankland contacted the Master G4[29] for assistance. The Master confirmed that there was no recovery company available. Lieutenant Colonel Frankland therefore instructed that all equipment that could not be brought under his control should be blown up on site so that it could not be recaptured by the enemy.*[30]

The inhabitants of La Gleize returned to the fields to discover a veritable cemetery of German vehicles.

Regarding the count of German casualties in the area, a report from the 30th ID Divisional Artillery states that twenty-three Panthers were captured in the village, probably including the two Panthers at Stoumont, the three at Targnon and the one at Cheneux. If there were seven Panzer IVs, the report counted eight Tigers in the area.[31]

This Hummel from SS-Panzer-Artillerie-Abteilung 1 was destroyed in Cooz on 20 December 1944 by Task Force *Lovelady*. (*Janco*)

After the battle in the Stavelot-La Gleize sector, a huge quantity of material was found abandoned. The 1. SS-Pz-Div lost a huge amount of equipment here. (*Jacobs Bibliothèque de Stavelot*)

A surprising piece of information when taking into account the six from La Gleize and Tiger 332 from Coo, which add up to seven in total. In this case, the inclusion of the Tiger from Petit Spay in the 117th Infantry Regiment's sector was also responsible for reducing the La Gleize pocket.

In any case, with this defeat the most advanced northern tip of the offensive was stopped. Without it, the chances of taking Antwerp and thus of achieving the objectives of the offensive were destroyed. This is why it is possible to say that if the Americans won the Battle of the Bulge at Bastogne, then the Germans lost it at La Gleize!

The Road to Bastogne

The situation report from von Rundstedt's OB West, dated 27 December 1944, also marks a clear change in the direction of operations. The German failure was now clear and it became imperative to evacuate the precious armoured troops who had ventured to the extreme west of the salient to avoid further catastrophe.

The 7. Armee proved unable to hold back Patton's thrust after reinforcements failed to arrive. Instead, it suffered the full force of the pressure of the Allied air force, its lines of communication expanding as the railway infrastructure deteriorated under the bombardment. Now it had to go to the other side of the Rhine to receive supplies and as the route for its trucks lengthened, the smallest crossroads were put under fire by American fighter-bombers, further aggravating the situation of its supplies.

The 5. Panzer-Armee placed itself in a defensive situation along the whole width of its front and was forced to withdraw its most advanced points. Von Manteuffel's HQ was

In the sector of the 5. Panzer-Armee, failure was just as obvious. This Panther Ausf G from 11. Panzer-Division was abandoned at Humain. (*NARA*)

A Sherman M4A3E8 from 4th Armored Division. These state-of-the-art Shermans were among those that opened the rescue corridor to Bastogne. (*NARA*)

now at Mont-le-Ban. The American breakthrough was reported to be only a 'schmale Gasse', a narrow road. General Karl Decker, commander of XXXIX Panzer-Korps, was in charge of the fighting around Bastogne and was to play an important role in the following days. The 3. Panzergrenadier-Division left Lommerweiler to put itself at von Manteuffel's disposal. The 167. Volksgrenadier-Division had already crossed the River Our with a regiment to join the general melee that was about to begin, with its vanguard in Noville.

The 6. Panzer-Armee increased its thrust on its left wing at Grandmenil and Erezée. On its right wing, 1. SS-Panzer-Division reorganised itself after the destruction of its KG Peiper at La Gleize and regrouped in the Born-Vielsalm-St Vith sector.[32] It was now very clear to all that Bastogne, which had just been opened up, was now the gravitational centre of the battle. In the eyes of the OKW, it was imperative to close the corridor Patton had just opened between this strategically important point and Neufchâteau. If the issue could be described as political, it was above all operational. The crossroads town of Bastogne was a springboard from which the Americans could hope to capture Houffalize. If this second important road junction was taken over by Patton's Third Army, the entire 5. Panzer-Armee was in danger of being caught in a huge trap from which it would only be able to get out in dribs and drabs.

The last surviving Panthers were lost north of Bastogne. (*NARA*)

Among this group of units, the shock division in charge of breaking through the right wing of the American corridor was 1. SS-Panzer-Division 'Leibstandarte Adolf Hitler', but the orders did not reach the division until the evening and it did not leave its assembly area until late in the afternoon the following day after having received more fuel.[33] It would take between 6 and 8 hours to arrive in the sector of the 5. Panzer-Armee.[34] The losses recorded during the first phase of the battle in the Stavelot-La Gleize sector had greatly reduced the offensive potential of the unit. The Gepanzerte Kampfgruppe of SS-Obersturmbannführer Peiper lost most of its equipment, including a large part of its Panthers. The armoured regiment was reconstituted as much as possible by gathering all the repaired equipment lost on the way to La Gleize. The division's HQ was set up for a time in the Schimpach station, but when it was burnt down by an air attack, Mohnke and his deputies set up camp in a nearby railway tunnel. Peiper remained with them in the rear throughout this phase of the battle and carried out staff duties. He was in no condition to take command and was in a miserable state.[35] Witnesses saw him at La Gleize leading the fight in cavalry boots, inappropriate footwear which must have caused him great pain as he escaped through the woods from the cauldron at La Gleize. He also twisted his foot when he slipped on a stone while crossing the Salm. Given its small numbers, the SS armoured division sent two Kampfgruppen to attack the American positions, KG Pötschke and KG Hansen. It seems that Monhke did not commit all his resources, as he still had sixteen Tiger IIs gathered in the Arloncourt-Harzy-Schimpach-Longvilly quadrilateral in the Kampfgruppe (KG) Möbius.[36] While

A 105-mm battery, the FH 18, found on the heights at Lutrebois. (*NARA*)

they were quick to see Tigers, even when there were none, American reports do not indicate the presence of any in the area.

SS-Sturmbannführer Werner Pötschke commanded the first KG, appropriately named KG Pötschke. He had at his disposal two Kompanie of SS-Panzer-Regiment 1. Blocked at Wanne and unable to venture westwards en masse, the 6. and 7. Kompanie with Panzer IVs suffered fewer losses. These tanks would take back Lutrebois to rush towards the US corridor. The assault was to fail in a genuine "killing ground" that left no chance for success. KG Hansen attacked further south and met stiff resistance from the 35th Infantry Division, but after initial successes, it also failed to break through.

The Tigers were later used as corps units and were no longer strictly within the 1. SS-Pz-Div.[37] At least two of them supported the attack of 9. SS-Pz-Div in the Vielsalm sector.

Meanwhile, several units were in the Bastogne sector, some of whom supported the Volksgrenadier-Division.

Between Noville and Bizory, the 340. Volksgrenadier-Division (VGD) surprised the 6th Armored Division with a vigorous attack on 3 January. It was to experience a bloody face-off in the sector for three days and suffered heavy losses from the American artillery. On the evening of 6 January, the 12. SS-Panzer-Division had to be relieved by order of the 6. Panzer-Armee. Its lines were taken over by the 340. VGD, which had already been severely weakened by its attacks in the previous days. An armoured group took up position behind it at Michamp and Obourcy.[38] This armoured group has two Tigers of the s. SS-Pz-Abt 501. and remained in the area until 12 January. One of the tanks was lost in circumstances that will be explained later. Another appeared to be on a similar mission for the 167. VGD, covering the withdrawal of SS-Pz-Div 1.

Machine gun nest of H Company, 137th Infantry Regiment, 35th Infantry Division, at Sainlez, early January 1945. (*NARA*)

A destroyed Panzer IV Ausf J in the Bastogne sector, near Lutrebois. (*NARA*)

Tigers of the s-SS-Panzer-Abteilung 501 protected the withdrawal of the I. SS-Panzer-Korps. This one was lost at Goronne. (*NARA*)

The last battle was in the sector of St Vith, where the Tiger Corps was once again confronted by the 30th ID. (*NARA*)

The main part of 1. SS-Panzer-Division was now in the sector of Tarchamp and started to withdraw in a north-easterly direction during the night of 9/10 January 1945. It would have to fight its way out of the Bastogne sector, via Clervaux, St Vith in order to reach the north of Cologne.[39] During the night of 14/15 January, the Stab of 6. Panzer-Armee was transferred to Rotgen, 5 kilometres south-south-east of St Vith. Its various units gathered their vehicles which had been abandoned for lack of fuel throughout the combat sector. However, only priority vehicles could be recovered as fuel was scarce.[40] It was therefore understandable that vehicles which had broken down or were difficult to recover were often abandoned to their sad fate.

On 15 January the SS division began to assemble in Cologne. Its fighters then left for Hungary, where they were practically exterminated. The division's last survivors were finally captured in Austria.

A Disastrous Balance Sheet

1. SS-Panzer-Division was dominated by its opponents both in the northern sector, where it had all its means at its disposal, and in the southern sector, where it faced an opponent in a precarious situation.

A destroyed Panther found by the 30th ID. (*NARA via 30th ID*)

The Chief of Staff of I. SS-Panzer-Korps explained the various reasons for this failure. The main thing, he said, was that the initial assault area was crossed by roads unsuitable for an armoured breakthrough, not to mention that the resistance of the American lines was much stronger than expected in the preparation of the offensive. I. SS-Panzer-Korps was also greatly disadvantaged by the lack of success of the neighbouring corps, LVVII Korps, which was unable to seize the Eischweiler and Butgenbach sectors and thus left the Americans with the opportunity to hold the roads north of the axis of advance, while in the south, the resistance of St Vith limited the freedom of movement of the German formations, giving the First US Army time to reinforce itself.

The German Chief of Staff also pointed out that the German divisions were less well trained than previously and that, in contrast, the American infantry units, systematically supported by a Tank Battalion and a Tank Destroyer Battalion, had a strength the German officers estimated to be equivalent to that of an armoured division.

Finally, the Allied air supremacy and the numerous logistical difficulties such as the lack of fuel, but also the lack of artillery ammunition, played strongly against the two Panzer armies.[41]

The SS division suffered enormous casualties. (*Jacobs Bibliothèque de Stavelot*)

Chapter 2

The Schwere SS-Panzer-Abteilung 501

A Brief History of the Unit

The first heavy tank battalion, the schwere SS-Panzer-Abteilung 101, was created within the Heer, the army of the Wehrmacht, on 10 May 1942.[1] This new unit was not intended to be included in an armoured division, but to be assigned to the higher echelon for specific missions where strong armoured support was required. The Tigers used in these units lacked the tactical mobility to be included in the Panzer divisions,[2] which were much more dynamic in their manoeuvrability.

In the Waffen-SS, the rule was initially a little different. The commanders of the SS-Panzer-Divisionen (SS-Pz-Div) did not see it the same way and advocated having a Tiger company within their armoured regiments. Their request was accepted and SS-Panzer-Regiment 'Leibstandarte Adolf Hitler' officially became part of the 4. schwere SS-Panzer-Kompanie (s-SS-Pz-Kp) on 24 December 1942. The SS-Pz-Div 'Das Reich' was given

Guderian insisted that the heavy tanks should be assembled in battalions and made available to units according to the needs of the front. (*NAC*)

The SS also demanded their own Tiger units. (*NARA*)

The interlocking road rollers required special attention. (*NARA*)

the same status and the 8. s-SS-Pz-Kp was integrated at the beginning of 1943. When in March 1943 the commanders of the two SS-Pz-Div. were informed that their heavy tank companies were to be taken away from them in order to concentrate their strike force in one battalion, they refused outright. As a result, they kept their precious beasts while the schwere SS-Panzer-Abteilung (s. SS-Pz-Abt) 101 was created by taking the personnel elsewhere. It was not until 19 July 1943 that the s. SS-Pz-Abt 101 was finally formed,[3] becoming part of the heavy company of the 'Leibstandarte' as the 3rd Kompanie.

The 88-mm long gun barrel was a real asset on the Russian front. (*NARA*)

The Staff of I. SS-Panzer-Korps (I. SS-Pz-Kp) was created on 27 July 1943, and was formed from the 'Hitlerjugend' and the cadres of 1. SS-Pz-Div 'Leibstandarte Adolf Hitler'. Josef 'Sepp' Dietrich was its first commander. The s. SS-Pz-Abt 101 joined the staff at Sennelager on 28

July 1943 for a period of training that lasted until 21 September, before leaving for the Beverloo camp in Belgium. On 4 August, the Tiger Is left for training at Mailly, in France. On 5 August 1943, the first commander of the battalion, SS-Sturmbannführer Heinz Von Westernhagen, was appointed. However, as he was convalescing from a serious wound, he did not take command of the unit until February 1944.

In August 1943, the division departed for northern Italy, where it stayed until mid-October. There it supported the 1. SS-Pz-Div. charged with disarming the surrendered Italian army and participating in anti-partisan actions.[4] On 28 October, the 1. and 2. Kompanie of Tiger I were transferred to SS-Panzer-Regiment 1 of the 'Leibstandarte Adolf Hitler', itself integrated into the 4. Panzer-Armee. The Staff Company and 3. Komp. were sent to Augustdorf, north of the Sennelager training camp.

Tanks decommissioned in Normandy were evacuated by rail, but not all of them reached their destination. (*NARA*)

The withdrawal meant travelling over several kimlometers, during which time many machines would break down. (*Rights reserved*)

On 1 January 1944, the s. SS-Pz-Abt 101 had 101 officers and 365 soldiers and NCOs, whereas the organisation chart provided for 180 officers and 419 soldiers and NCOs. Only nine Tiger Is were operational.[5] On 9 January 1944, the battalion was transferred to the Mons region in Belgium, where training continued.

On 20 March, the crews who had been transferred to the Eastern Front returned and the unit was finally almost organically complete. SS-Hauptsturmführer[6] Rudolf Möbius took over the reins of 1. Komp., while SS-Obersturmführer[7] Michael Wittmann took over the leadership of 2. Komp.

At the beginning of April 1944, the armoured unit moved to the region of Beauvais to prepare for the Allied invasion that strategists of the Third Reich were expecting in the Pas de Calais region.

By 1 June, thirty-seven Tiger Is and one Bergepanther[8] were operational.[9] On 7 June, the day after the Allied landings, the heavy tank battalion of I. SS. Pz-Kp. set off for Normandy, that same day crossing Paris and passing under the Arc de Triomphe. By 8 June, movement began to become more difficult due to the Allied fighter-bombers firing on all potential targets, and by 9 June, movement was only possible at night because of the Allied air threat. On 10 June 2, s. SS-Pz-Abt 101 arrived in Falaise during the night. Under cover of darkness, 1. and 2. Komp. reached their assembly areas on 12 June, with 1. s. SS-Pz-Abt 101 8 kilometres north-east of Villers-Bocage on the N175, and Michael Wittmann's 2. s. SS-Pz-Abt 101 assembled in a pass south of Montbrocq,[10] before being immediately ordered to cover the left flank. The length of the move was very expensive for the armoured formation: only eight Tiger Is arrived from 1. s. SS-Pz-Abt 101. It was worse for 2. s. SS-Pz-Abt 101, where only six Tiger Is were present.[11] However, all of s. SS-Pz-Abt 101 entered the battle of Normandy with great fanfare, and the survivors of 2. s. SS-Pz-Abt 101 put out of action a good part of the famous 7th British Armoured Division, the famous 'Desert Rats'.

From 28 July onwards, the Tiger Is were gradually replaced by Tiger IIs. The s. SS-Pz-Abt 101 fought relentlessly, ceding ground step by step throughout the Normandy campaign, wiping out a considerable amount of equipment, mainly from the British Empire forces.

On 4 September Rolf Mobius reached the banks of the Meuse at Huy with only two Tigers. The next day, only one Tiger continued on its way to Germany, while the other surviving Tiger was abandoned due to lack of fuel and sabotaged. In mid-September the survivors were gathered in the Düren area and on the 22nd, the battalion was integrated

Tiger 113 was lost during the retreat to Jemappe. (*WHI*)

into and renamed schwere SS-Panzer-Abteilung 501, being re-equipped entirely with Tiger IIs. However, it was high time it received reinforcements – on 17 October 1944 it had only four tanks. It received two more the next day but had to wait until 11 November to receive eight more, and the same number a fortnight later. From one delivery to the next, the Abteilung reached its planned quota of forty-five heavy tanks on 4 December. On 13 December, the heavy tanks arrived in the assembly area at Tondorf for the Battle of the Bulge.[12] After the failure in the Amblève Valley, about fifteen Tiger IIs took the direction of the front in Bastogne under the authority of Rolf Mobius. The s. SS-Pz-Abt 501 ended its career on the Eastern Front on 9 May 1945.

The losses of the heavy battalion amounted to 107 Tiger I and Tiger II tanks: 31 percent were destroyed by their crew, 67 percent destroyed in action and 2 percent were unknown.[13] The ratio of tanks lost to destroyed was 1:4.7.[14]

A Band of Wild Animals

As of 16 December, the unit was constituted as follows:

The Stab:
The three Stab tanks were:

Tank Commander No. **007** – SS-Obersturmbannführer Heinz von Westernhagen
Deputy Tank No. **008** – SS-Untersturmführer Eduard Kalinowsky
Signals Officer Tank No. **009** – SS-Obersturmführer Wilhelm Dollinger

The numbers on the turret were in yellow ochre with grey edging.

1. **Kompanie:**
   Company Commander No. **105** – SS-Obersturmführer Jürgen Wessel
   Tank No. **104** – SS-Oberscharführer Joseph Franzl

   1. Zug **(Section)**
   Tank No. **111 (Zugführer)** – SS-Untersturmführer Rolf Henniges
   Tank No. **112** – SS-Oberscharführer Hein Bode
   Tank No. **113** – SS-Oberscharführer Fritz Zahner
   Tank No. **114** – SS-Oberscharführer Helmut Fritsche

   2. Zug **(Section)**
   Tank No. **121** – SS-Untersturmführer Heinz Buchner
   Tank No. **122** – SS-Oberscharführer Paul Steinwender
   Tank No. **123** – SS-Oberscharführer Franz Staudegger
   Tank No. **124** – SS-Oberscharführer Arno Salamon

3. Zug **(Section)**
Tank No. **131** – SS-Oberscharführer Jurgen Brandt (Cap)
Tank No. **132** – SS-Unterscharführer Willi Otterbein
Tank No. **133** – SS-Oberscharführer Werner Wendt
Tank No. **134** – SS-Unterscharführer Helmut Dannleitner

For the fourteen Panzers of the first company, the numbers painted on the turret were, in theory, yellow/orange with a grey border.

2. **Kompanie:**
   Company Commander No. **205** – SS-Hauptsturmführer Rolf Möbius
   Staff **204** – SS-Unterscharführer Eduard Stadler

1. Zug **(Section)**
Tank No. **211** – SS-Oberscharführer Wilhelm Dollinger (No. **009**), replaced by Paul Klose
Tank No. **212** – SS-Unterscharführer Franz Faustmann
Tank No. **213** – SS-Unterscharführer Ludwig Eser
Tank No. **214** – Unknown

2. Zug **(Section)**
Tank No. **221** – SS-Oberscharführer Georg Hantusch
Tank No. **222** – SS-Unterscharführer Kurt Sowa
Tank No. **223** – SS-Unterscharführer Walter Müller
Tank No. **224** – SS-Unterscharführer Grätzer

3. Zug **(Section)**
Tank No. **231** – SS-Untersturmführer Walther Hahn
Tank No. **232** – SS-Unterscharführer Ewald Mölly
Tank No. **233** – SS-Hauptscharführer Georg Lötzsch
Tank No. **234** – SS-Oberscharführer Matten

The numbers painted on the turret of the tanks of the second company were, in theory, black with a white border.

3. **Kompanie**
   Company Commander No. **305** – SS-Hauptsturmführer Heinz Birnschein
   Staff No. **304** – Unknown

1. Zug **(Section)**
Tank No. **311** – SS-Untersturmführer Thomas Amselgruber
Tank No. **312** – SS-Oberscharführer Heinrich Ritter

Tank No. **313** – SS-Hauptscharführer Peter Kisters
Tank No. **314** – Unknown

2. Zug **(Section)**
Tank No. **321** – SS-Hauptscharführer Winfried Lukasius
Tank No. **322** – SS-Unterscharführer Herbst
Tank No. **323** – SS-Oberscharführer Fritz Renfordt
Tank No. **324** – Unknown

3. Zug **(Section)**
Tank No. **331** – SS-Hauptscharführer Rolf von Westernhagen
Tank No. **332** – SS-Unterscharführer Otto Blase
Tank No. **333** – SS-Oberscharführer Heimo Traue
Tank No. **334** – Unknown

The colour of the numbers painted on the turret was, in theory, blue with a yellow border.

In the list of the thirty best tank killers of the entire Panzerwaffe (Heer and SS combined), several armoured combat aces belonged to s-SS-Panzer-Abteilung 501.

- #5 was Michael Wittmann, the darling of Nazi propaganda, who scored 138 victories. Wittmann was killed in action in Normandy on 8 August 1944, on the road between Caen and Falaise.
- #6 Karl Möbius: 125 registered victories.
- #14 Helmut Wendorff: 84 registered victories.
- #16 'Bobby Woll': 80 registered victories. Bobby was Michael Wittmann's gunner and close friend.
- #24 Karl Warmbrunn: 57 registered victories.
- #25 Heinz Kling: 51 registered victories.
- #26 Jürgen Brandt: 51 victories. Brandt commanded Tiger 131 in the Peiper offensive and would destroy his last tanks near the bridge of Petit Spay. Brandt blew up his tank before being fatally hit by shrapnel during the withdrawal of Knittel's troops.

The record of these seven tank commanders impressive: 586 victories. So many vehicles and anti-tank guns turned into piles of smoking scrap metal.

Chapter 3

Tigers Lost between the Start Line and Stavelot

On the Way to the Frontline

The rise of the unit was not only linked to the perception of its equipment. Its crews were reinforced by new recruits who had to be trained in an atmosphere of scarcity. Werner Wendt, commander of Tiger 133, explained: '*Training is given on the equipment, but due to a shortage of fuel and ammunition, there is no target practice. From 1 to 3 December, the detachment moved by rail to the south-east of Cologne. The Flak and reconnaissance platoons remained behind in the former barracks, as they were not yet re-equipped.*'[1]

On the night of 13/14 December, the heavy tanks arrived in the assembly area on both sides of the road to Zingsheim and Engelgau, while the detachment's headquarters were set up in Tondorf. The first echelon and the kitchen truck were in the assembly area. The element of surprise needed to be preserved and it was vital the heavy tanks and their crews were as inconspicuous as possible. Drastic stealth measures were therefore taken. Coffee could only be prepared at night, and all movement was strictly forbidden during the day.

The s. Panzer-Abteilung 506 would also fight in the Ardennes and was able to practise target shooting, which the 501 was unable to do. (*Tegethoff*)

Tiger 222 seen crossing through Tondorf. (*NARA*)

The first part of the journey was made by train to protect the tank's fragile mechanics. (*Tegethoff*)

At Lanzeradt, the first US prisoners of the 99th Infantry Division are marched towards Germany, while Tiger 222 advances towards its fate. (NARA)

Wendt explained in 1991 that:

> *During the night of 15 December, the company commander briefed the platoon leaders on the objectives to be attacked in the next few days and also pointed out that Skorzeny's men had been assigned to a specific sector. The platoon leaders then gave their instructions to the tank commanders. On 16 December, the companies remained in the assembly areas for some time, sometimes up to twelve hours or more. The marching order was as follows: 2nd Company, Staff, 3rd Company and 1st Company.*[2]

Tiger 222 was the most photographed as it moved out of the column and met the Propaganda Kompagnie, who made it a star. (*NARA*)

Our investigation has allowed us to identify seventeen of the forty-five Tiger IIs of schwere SS-Panzer-Abteilung 501 in the Stavelot-La Gleize sector and two in the Bastogne sector. Only one probably managed to escape, the other eleven being abandoned. For an easier understanding of their history, their fate is presented here in chronological order.

It was not until 0900hrs on 17 December that the machines emerged from Route 421 at the junction with the 265, heading in the direction of Losheimergraben. Honsfeld was crossed around noon, almost 12 hours after the Peiper Spitze. According to Wendt:

> *During the night of 17 December, we left the assembly area of Tondord-Blankenheim by roads overloaded with heavy traffic. The lead detachment followed the head of the tank column to Bullange. Tanks isolated by breakdowns or stragglers could be directed on diversionary routes and this was the case for tanks 202 and 203. All tanks in marching order continued to follow the head of the long armoured column. Six to eight paratroopers perched on each tank accompanied us. There was no engagement with the enemy on 17 December 1944.*[3]

The Tiger was a mechanically delicate vehicle, whose transmission was notoriously undersized for the machine's weight (70 tonnes) and thus the tracks were under a great deal of pressure. During the Battle of the Bulge, moving the machines posed a real problem. The roads they had to use were winding and rough, and the fragile mechanics of the Tiger suffered greatly. Several broke down because of transmission failures, whereby they would be overtaken by the others and sometimes quickly put back on the road. Machines in need of heavy repair were evacuated to the rear and assembled in Engelsdorf.

The orderly arrangement of the companies was severely disrupted. For example, Tank 222 was the last to arrive in front of the Stavelot bridge because it had lost its way and passed through Kaiserbaracke. These disruptions explain why machines from the three companies and the Stab were to be found on the other side of the Amblève, even though they represented only 30 percent of the total strength of the Abteilung. We counted one machine belonging to the staff, four from 1. Komp., five from 2. Komp. and two from 3. Komp.

As a general rule, routes to the front should preferably be taken slowly. To avoid breakdowns, the first stop should ideally be after 5 kilometres and then every 10-15 kilometres. It was preferable for heavy vehicles to use soft ground, as roads wore out the rubber rings of the inner rollers very quickly.

Despite the precautions taken, mechanical problems were already occurring frequently and were to multiply in the Ardennes, with the aggravating fact that the maintenance units would not be able to intervene at the front of the column while it was in contact with the enemy.

Tiger 131: Victim of the Jabos

Captain Peterson took his 506th Fighter Squadron, equipped with P47 Thunderbolts, on a mission in the Euskirchen area between the frontline and the Rhine. His eleven aircraft were to attack truck convoys as part of the US doctrine to isolate the battlefield by cutting off lines of communication.

Halfway to the target area, Peterson received a call from 'Roselee', the ground controller, who instructed him to ignore his orders and attack a concentration of trucks and vehicles at point K-6801, whose coordinates corresponded to the village of Coo. Peterson hurriedly checked his map, asking for confirmation of the message as K-6801 was 25 miles inside US lines. The ground controller validated the instructions. Visibility on the ground being practically zero and almost impossible for operational flight over the village, the group continued on to Stavelot at 1515hrs, where a clearing finally broke through the cloud cover. Five thousand feet below, stretching along a narrow pass on the side of a steep hill, was a column of tanks and trucks estimated at about forty vehicles.[4] There was panic on the ground before the fighter-bombers began strafing with their

The Thunderbolts were responsible for the loss of Tiger 131. (*NARA*)

The straffing of the Allied airmen was only just countered by the available Flak. (*Jacobs Bibliothèque de Stavelot*)

Browning 50s, as the SS rushed to the shelter of the houses in the Rue du Vieux Château. During the dawn attack, one tank, Panther 115 of SS-Panzer-Regiment 1, was knocked out of action by a US 76.2-mm towed gun and remained frozen in the spot where Uncle Sam's shell had hit it. When the air raid alert was triggered, SS-Oberscharführer Jürgen Brandt's

Tiger 131 stopped at the wreckage and the crew took refuge in a nearby house. His vehicle was attacked by fighter-bombers, who shot at the rear deck of the vehicle. As the fighter-bombers moved away, a thick plume of black smoke rose from the Tiger. The road was blocked and after about an hour, the driver managed to restart the tank. Unfortunately, the tank stopped again a few metres further on, which was enough to clear the road. Brandt was impatient and could not wait for the recovery company. Instead, the Panzerführer took his place in the tank that followed him, No. 132. The commander of 132, Willi Otterbein, did not want to be left behind either, and so simply ejected the radio and took its place in the vehicle. The aircraft was followed by Tiger 133 as it descended towards Stavelot. On 25 December, Tiger 131 could not be repaired and had to be abandoned; its exposed position on the ledge above Stavelot preventing any possible recovery attempts. The German divisions that took over the sector from I. SS-Pz-Kp, the 18. Volksgrenadier-Division and 3. Fallschirmjäger-Division did not have the equipment to recover a machine of this size.

Fallschirmjäger of 3. FJD climb aboard the tanks. The American air attacks would cause great losses in their ranks. (*NARA*)

Tiger 105: A Bull in a China Shop

Commissioned by SS-Obersturmführer Wessel, the first Tiger lost by the schwere SS-Panzer-Abteilung 501 bore the number 105. In the late morning of 18 December, Peiper was already several kilometres away with some of the 2. and 3. Kompanien. To his rear, 1. Kompanie crossed Stavelot in the afternoon in order to join him. Unfortunately for the Germans, the American pressure in the streets of the town was increasing, and the bazookas of the 117th Infantry Regiment of the 30th Infantry Division were waiting

Our investigation determined the location of the 825th Tank Destroyer Battalion (Towed). The wreckage of this Jeep, photographed in Stavelot, attests to the unit's presence in the town. (*Jacobs Bibliothèque de Stavelot*)

for the Panzers halfway up the coast, while the main road was under fire from anti-tank guns. The German column could no longer pass along this route up from the bridge, forcing Wessel to take a narrower, parallel road. It was now around 1500hrs. When the road reached its end, a GI fired a rocket from a house window at the tank, forcing it to turn back and run into a building below. This version seems to be corroborated by the report of the 825th Tank Destroyer Battalion, which was armed with 3-inch guns: '*About 15 rounds were exchanged during the fight. One of the shells fired from a 3' struck the tank at the mantelet and it fell back. In doing so, the tank ran into a house and became trapped under the rubble.*'[5] This report was written more than two weeks after the battle. However, it has long been taken at face value. Especially as the photographs in our possession show an impact on the right of the mantle. Nevertheless, several details allow us to discredit this thesis. Indeed, Wessel contradicts this version as, according to him, the blow to the mantelet occurred before he crossed the Amblève and entered the street that would prove fatal. Here is his testimony:

Jürgen Wessel's testimony confirms that Tiger 105 was hit in its hull. (*Jacobs Bibliothèque de Stavelot*)

> *The main part of the Kampfgruppe "Peiper", the 2. Kompanie and the staff of the Abteilung had already crossed Stavelot. I approached the town with 1. Kompanie. I was in the lead. Just before the bridge over the Amblève, I received a blow in the hull. As the gun was no longer usable, I went full throttle over the bridge and soon arrived at a crossroads, where we received two rounds in the front. I gave the order to move back, and the Panzer ran into the wall of a house. It collapsed and rubble fell on my armour. The crew and I evacuated. The next Tiger of the Kompanie was under the command of SS-Oberscharführer Brand. He was coming up behind me. I gave him the order to destroy the anti-tank* [gun] *and got into another Panzer.*[6] *I went full speed through Stavelot to link up with the front. Unfortunately, my Kompanie could not follow me, and I could not turn back because the enemy had reinforced the town in the meantime. The Kompanie was not able to join the Kampfgruppe "Peiper" afterwards.*[7]

This was not the only element that casts doubt on the version that has been commonly accepted for years. Tiger 105 crossed the town after the other two companies in the afternoon. However, the US report states that 825th Tank Destroyer Battalion evacuated the town at 1145hrs, well before the Panzer arrived. If it was not them, then another unit was responsible for the disabling of the town.

Close-up of the pierced hull (circled). (*Jacobs Bibliothèque de Stavelot*)

The attack by infantrymen of the 30th ID, reinforcing those of the 526th Armored Infantry Battalion, forced Wessel to retreat. (*NARA*)

In the afternoon of 18 December, only four M10s belonging to the 823rd Tank Destroyer Battalion were present, having arrived around 1300hrs to support the infantrymen of the 117th Infantry Regiment, who were sent to take back the town. In the early afternoon they were on the northern heights of Stavelot, at the place called Haute Levée. From there, the Tank Destroyers had an excellent firing position to block the road approaching the bridge from the east, on the other side of the valley. After checking the evidence at the location, it was probably them who hit Wessel's tank.

In order to be certain, the feasibility of the event from a ballistic point of view still needed to be verified. The M10 was equipped with the M7 version of the 3-inch Anti-Tank Gun, which could fire two types of armour-piercing rounds. The M79 was a conventional AP,[8] its perforating capacity being 70 mm of superficially hardened steel at a distance of 914 metres.[9] However, at this time of the conflict, the M10s were equipped with the M62A1 head, an APC filled with 0.652 kg of ammonium picrate, a high explosive. The detonation of the charge took place just after impact. As a result of such a blow, the recoil damping system of the 88-mm gun was irreparably destroyed. After a quick calculation based on the in-situ measurement of the machine's hull, which is still at La Gleize today, we have determined that at this point the thickness was 134 mm. Taking into account the fact that the impact was vertical, the firing tables of the 3-inch M62A1 shell reveal that a perforation of the firing chamber was possible up to a distance of 1,550 metres. The After Action Report highlighted the engagement with German tanks coming from the west and east of Stavelot. A destruction of eight to ten Panzers was claimed: a majority of Panthers and some Tigers. Although the number of victories was exaggerated, the report attests to the fact that one engagement against Tiger guns that afternoon went well. According to a witness, when the machine was evacuated a crew member was hit in the head, while the loader was wounded in the abdomen. The reason for this was that the hit on the target, shortly before the bridge, caused the ammunition in the chamber to fire unexpectedly, thus causing the cannon to recoil and hit the fighter.

In his testimony, SS-Obersturmführer Jürgen Wessel mentions that he was hit twice on the front of the tank. Close observation of the photographs reveals that there is no

This tank has ended up in the front of a building on Rue Haut-Rivage. (*Jacobs Bibliothèque de Stavelot*)

This photograph shows the ventilation outlets on the rear deck were completely blocked. (*Jacobs Bibliothèque de Stavelot*)

trace of bazooka impact. There is, on the other hand, a testimony from a GI of the 526th Armored Infantry. A sergeant of the heavy platoon, armed with a 60-mm mortar, fired at the big tank and claimed to have hit it, even causing it to reverse backwards down the steep street and crash into a house. A 60-mm mortar shell was unable to pierce the armour of a Tiger, even if the top of the tank was hit, but in the darkness that falls early at that time of the year, the "flash" of the bazooka or mortar was visible. If the mortar impact was ineffective, the slamming of the shot on the armour would have been no less impressive and could have been mistaken for an anti-tank shell, which consequently resulted in the order to turn back.

The turret number 105 can just be made out in this picture. (*NARA*)

In view of all these elements, the facts can be reconstructed as follows: at the head of 1. Kompanie, Tiger 105 was the target of an anti-tank weapon shortly before the bridge, and was hit in the mantelet. A high-explosive shell was in the chamber, which exploded under the impact of the projectile. The violent recoil of the 88-mm shot hit the outfitter Neuman in the stomach by surprise, who then collapsed, writhing in pain, at the bottom of the turret. The gun was no longer usable. Under stress, the tank commander ordered the tank to go full throttle to cross the river. Instructions were given for the tank not to take the widest street straight ahead, but to head to the left and then up the street. As it passed over the street, just before turning left, the tank was targeted and two shots crashed into its upper part, where the armour was less thick. The officer shouted into the intercom: 'Zurück! Zurück!'[10] With the tank almost at a standstill, the driver shifted into reverse, down the slippery slope,[11] soon losing control of the monster, which fell backwards. The driver must have reversed the levers to drive forward again, as a howl of tormented sprockets and chainrings was heard. Very soon afterwards, it came to a sudden stop and there was a terrifying noise; the Tiger had crashed into the front of a building, which proceeded to collapse on top of it. As the rubble of the building piled up on the

Photographed in the spring of 1945, the BOSCH headlight has already been dismantled. (*Jacobs Bibliothèque de Stavelot*)

rear deck, the monster's engine was muffled, and the crew only managed to extricate themselves from the vehicle with great effort.

Indeed, the *Tigerfibel*, the training manual for Tiger crews, emphasised obstacle negotiation. Although a Pz.Kpf. VI had enough power to destroy a building without any problem, it was recommended not to break through walls as the resulting dust would instantly clog the air filters and radiator fins, causing the engine to choke or inevitably overheat.[12] In addition to fuel, an engine needs a supply of air for combustion, and if the engine in question was a Maybach HL230 V-twelve with 700 horsepower at 3,000 rpm, this represented a theoretical intake flow of more than 1m^3 per second. This amount of air had to be filtered and warmed up before it was injected into the huge carburettor. Before entering the carburettor, the air was purified via two successive filter stages consisting of an oil bath, which captured impurities by hydrostatic effect as the intake air touched the interface with the oil. The flow then passed through a membrane filter before being

The US slings broke during the first attempt to free the tank, after the M10s who were to pull it tore the cables. (*NARA*)

admitted to the carburettor. The Maybach was equipped with a battery of three such filters, one for every four cylinders. As the Tiger absorbed almost 1m^3 of air per second, it acted like a high-powered vacuum cleaner, capable of fulfilling the dreams of the most demanding housewife… In addition, tarpaulins, luggage, tree leaves and rubble had to be removed from the rear deck so that they did not interfere with the air flow and the rotation of the turret.

By this time, Hans Neuman was no longer screaming in pain, but rather groaning as he lay there, unconscious. The evacuation of the tank was decided. Wessel's testimony is also very instructive from an operational point of view as it explains why Peiper was cut off from the rest of his Kampfgruppe. Furthermore, it provides an insight into the reason why Tiger 132 never managed to reach Peiper.

The story of Tiger 105 does not end there. After retaking the town, some GIs had the idea of towing the monster so that the 88-mm shells could be returned to sender. An M10 anti-tank tried to fire the armour embedded in the facade without success. A second M10 was called in to help pull the Tiger II out of the rubble, but their efforts were also in vain when the towing cable broke. Tiger 105 remained in place, and a piece

The tank was not finally removed from the Rue Haut-Rivage until the following summer. (*Jacobs Bibliothèque de Stavelot*)

of the broken steel sling is visible in a photograph. Its weight, 70 tonnes in running order, was certainly an obstacle to towing, and was made even more difficult by the rubble on and around the tank. The fragile gearbox had also given up the ghost. In an understandable reflex, the driver must have tried to re-engage the forward gear by reversing the lever (the direction of the first four gears can be reversed by operating a single lever). After the war, Tiger 105 was not scrapped on site because of the risk of the building collapsing. Instead, it was towed to be stored on the Trois-Ponts road about 400 metres from the Antoine Farm.[13]

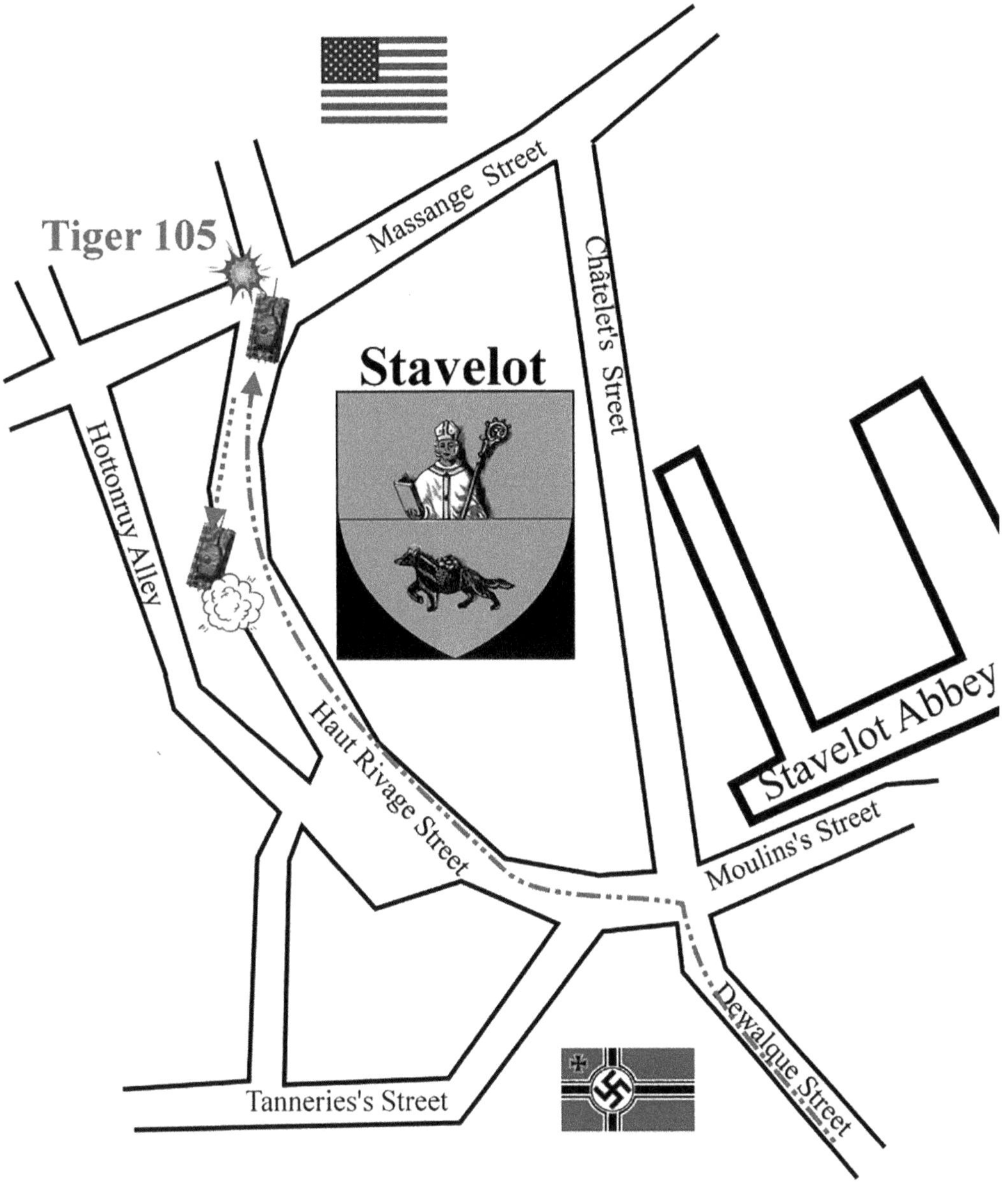

Map showing the route of Tiger 105. (*Authors' collection*)

Tigers 132 and 133: The Gemini of Petit Spay

As mentioned above, the heavy tanks were only to be deployed after the crossing of the Meuse, near Amay. The assembly area was not defined. The tanks' progress was made as smoothly as possible according to the amenities and hazards encountered on the way. The three Tigers, from the same section, travelled together. The Zugführer, SS-Oberscharführer Jürgen Brandt, an ace of the Panzerwaffe with a score of fifty enemy tanks was on board Tiger 131. Tiger 132 followed, commanded by SS-Unterscharführer

The Hotel des Ardennes in Ligneuville housed the US headquarters when Peiper's armoured spike appeared. (*NARA*)

Willi Otterbein. Finally, Tiger 133, commanded by SS-Oberscharführer Werner Wendt, brought up the rear. Tiger 134, the fourth tank of the platoon, was apparently further back in the column.

In the afternoon of 18 December, Tiger 132, commanded by SS-Oberscharführer Brandt, followed by Wendt's Tiger 133, were the last two big cats to cross Stavelot. Directly behind Wessel, Brandt learned that an enemy gun was protecting the approaches to the bridge and so ordered them to charge. In his account, Wendt says:

> *On the morning of 18 December, the first company was attacked by about eight twin-engine bombers in the area of Thirimont-Baugnez. No tanks or other vehicles were lost, but there were casualties among the paratroopers. On this 18th December, at about 1030hrs, we stopped for a long time at Ligneuville in front of an abandoned American HQ.*
>
> *The battle-ready tanks of the second and third companies crossed Stavelot at about this time. The first company reached the heights of Stavelot at around 0100hrs. It had to clear the road to let through parts of Sturmbanführer Knittel's reconnaissance detachment. The road was under heavy bombardment from enemy artillery. At 1500hrs Obersturmführer Wessel and a second Tiger crossed the bridge over the Amblève.*[14]

Tigers 132 and 133 took the Hottonruy alley, which was so narrow that they tore off parts of the facade. (*Jacobs Bibliothèque de Stavelot*)

Obersturmführers Brandt and Wendt, as an additional tank force, then moved towards the bridge. As they crossed it, both tanks were attacked by a fighter-bomber. Brandt's tank was damaged in its tracks and suspension and had to stop 30 metres from the bridge. The repair of Brandt's tank took a long time and because of the narrowness of the street, no tanks could pass by, meaning Wendt, who was following, was blocked behind him. Night soon fell, meaning both crews had to spend the night in Stavelot. From where they stood the night appeared calm. Only a few cyclists could pass by, their bicycles squeezing in between the immobilised Tigers and the facades of the narrow street.[15]

The situation was no better for the rest of 1. Kompanie, whose commander was at La Gleize, cut off from his unit. III. Zug was partly blocked in the last passable street allowing access across the town from the bridge. If I. and II. Zug arrived behind it, they would find themselves in a monster traffic jam in the middle of the firing range. Faced

Sturmbannführer Gustav Knittel (right) with his deputy Walter Leidreiter photographed between Lodomez and Lavaux-Richard, shortly before the Thunderbolt attack. (*NARA*)

with this potential disaster, the rest of the Tiger IIs did not venture onto the bridge until the town was cleared. This meant that they stayed behind and were therefore of no use to Peiper.

On 19 December, as dawn was breaking at around 0730hrs, the tanks of Brandt and Wendt set off again towards Trois-Ponts. They took over Wessel's crew, whose tank was stuck under the debris of the house it had rammed. The tanks' undercarriages suffered terribly trying to get the vehicles out of the town. Before the first crossroads, the road narrowed and the tracks scraped along the facades.[16] Two kilometres beyond Stavelot, the two Tigers arrived at the KG command post of Sturmbannführer Knittel, who knew nothing about the general situation. The two Tigers stayed there and around 1000hrs, Knittel ordered them to return to Stavelot to see what was going on there. Wendt explains how they were not able to fulfil their mission: '*We did not go far because all kinds of mines had been laid on the road at the edge of Stavelot. Meanwhile, it was clear that Stavelot had been taken over by the enemy.*'[17]

Throughout the night of 18/19 December, Stavelot was on fire. The men of 2. Kompanie, SS-Aufklärungs-Abteilung 1 fought in the town to try to reopen the main road up from the Amblève. They did not succeed.

Major General Leland S. Hobbs' 30th Infantry Division ('Old Hickory') was called in and burst into the town. Throughout the Western European campaign this division was supported by Major Philips' 743rd Tank Battalion. The history of the armoured unit describes the mood of its ranks as it moved to the front:

A Panzergrenadier shot down at the southern entrance to Stavelot square during the fighting on 18 December. (*Rights reserved*)

Through Malmedy and Stavelot, the best troops the Nazis had – the 1st SS Adolf Hitler Division – were heading for Spa and Liège. It was up to the 30th Division and attached units to collide with the SS and stop them. Major Philips summarises the situation as the tanks awaited orders on the road to Malmedy. The company commanders had been placed at the head of the column. Major Philips had a map of the area and spread it on the front plate of the staff tank and informed the officers all he knew about the enemy positions. "This", the Major summed up, "is another Mortain for us. I don't like it any more than you do, but it's history. It is our job to meet the enemy, stop him, hold him and destroy him."

Then the company commanders were given their assignments. […] *VERIFY*[18] *had reached the Ardennes and for the next week of action everything was going to be a strange and somewhat mad affair. There was an entirely new feeling in the fighting. After months of offensive action, with the German armies swept away and the end thought to be in sight, men suddenly found themselves on the defensive fighting for their lives. The gravity of the situation is not to be underestimated. The strangest thing was the almost total lack of information. The wildest rumours appeared… The Germans had cut the roads north of Malmedy… The Germans had reached Liège… The Germans had dropped parachutists and were fighting in Antwerp… The Germans were having huge successes… The only thing the Battalion could be certain of when it went into action in Belgium was that it would face the 1st SS Panzer Division – the same nominal division it had faced and defeated at Mortain. After its defeat in France, the 1st SS was reformed and re-equipped. This was the return battle. There had been vague situations before, but none as mystifying*

Shermans breaking through the Ardennes. (*NARA*)

> *as this. Some platoon leaders received maps of the area, but others did not receive them until several days after the fighting had started. For those who had to travel the steep, winding roads without maps, it was like groping in the dark, often not knowing whether the road was in friendly or enemy territory. Tanks and platoons were soon scattered to the four winds, ready to hold vital roadblocks.*

On 19 December, 743rd Tank Battalion had its tanks assigned to infantry units and was deployed in and around Malmedy-Stavelot. Control of Stavelot had to be regained. Baker Company of the 743rd supported the infantrymen of the 117th Infantry Regiment of the Old Hickory.[19]

For the Americans, holding the bridge was just as vital. Captain Leland Cofer, commander of A Company, 105th Engineer Battalion, provided an account of his mission to blow up the bridge in order to cut off the Tigers' route and prevent them from reaching Peiper:

The SS break through the lines and arrive as reinforcements. (*NARA*)

At that time I was a platoon leader in Able of the 105th Engineer Battalion, part of the 30th ID. Our division was just north of Aachen, in Germany, and west of the Roer River, where the front had been static for about six weeks. On 17 December we were detached from the Ninth Army and reassigned to the First Army. At the end of the day we set off southwards on tracks crowded with moving troops. For much of the night we were harassed by the Luftwaffe, who sent up lots of flares but few bombs. Several armored and infantry divisions were directed into the Ardennes to counter the German offensive. By the end of the day, on 18 December, the 1st Battalion of the 117th Infantry Regiment, to which our engineer company was attached, had attacked the town of Stavelot and was pushing the enemy back to the bridge over the river. The bridge, still intact, was the only one for several miles. If the Germans were to continue their offensive, they had to take and protect it so that their troops could cross the natural obstacle to take Liège and Antwerp, their original objectives. At about noon on Tuesday, 19 December, I received orders to go to Stavelot and destroy the bridge. Reconnaissance being the first thing to be done, I set off in my Jeep driven by my T-5 driver, Tony Barone. He drove me as close as possible to the river in the Jeep, then I went the rest of the way on foot, arriving at the frontline held by the guys of the 117th. The line ran along the river, the infantrymen having taken up their positions in the houses, upstairs and downstairs. The Jerries occupied the south side of the river, with a tank and infantry covering the bridge. The bridge itself was in No Man's Land.

GIs from 117th Infantry Regiment in the Stavelot area. (*NARA*)

During the day, it would have been suicidal to venture out in full view of the enemy. It was essential that I had a view of the bridge to see its structure in order to assess what action was needed to destroy it. With maximum caution, moving from house to house, I came to a first-storey window, where I had a good view of the bridge but remained invisible. I sketched out the bridge and estimated the length of the spans and the thickness of the deck. There was an abandoned US Army Jeep on the bridge and the body of a soldier wearing the uniform of an armored unit…

We returned to company headquarters, which was on the hill from where our troops had arrived. There I planned and organised a demolition team. We did not have access to the underside of the bridge to destroy it, as recommended by the pioneer school. An excessive amount of TNT was estimated, as the charge was to be placed on the bridge deck: 1,000 pounds (454 kg) divided into 20 boxes of 50 pounds (23 kg) which would be placed on the ground. Three slow-burning fuses connected to the detonators were used . This was twice as much as was needed, but I wanted to guarantee the explosion. To prevent the Germans from retaking the bridge, our action had to be carried out as quickly as possible. We planned this as soon as it was dark, agreeing with the artillery that they would fire high-explosive shells and other smoke at a constant rate.

The explosive shells were to drown out the noise of our demolition action, while the smoke and darkness made us invisible to the enemy. Firing was to start at the agreed time, but I soon forgot what this was, it must have been 7 or 8 o'clock in the evening. The TNT and men were loaded into 6X6 trucks and with my Jeep we drove down the hill. When

The Stavelot bridge was blown up after 2000hrs on 19 December. The US engineers put their charges under the first span on the side of the abbey. (*Jacobs Bibliothèque de Stavelot*)

we got close to the structure, we waited for the artillery fire. Before we went into action, a French-speaking soldier went to check if people were still in the houses near the bridge, but I don't remember if we found anyone. I think they had evacuated the town during the initial fighting. When the first shells fell, the men each took a case of TNT. We had rubber soled shoes, but the broken windows shattered by the fighting squealed horribly under our feet and we seemed to be making a hell of a noise. Staff Sergeant James McKeon (who was killed a month later) and Sergeant Lowell Richardson from the 117th IR accompanied us and helped to place the TNT crates on the thinnest part of the first span. The men put down their crates and ran back to the truck, McKeon, Richardson and I pulled the three fuses and lit them with the famous lighter, which works even in high winds. We took off

The thick walls of the old Stavelot Abbey sheltered the heavy machine guns of D Coy, 117th IR, who held the bridge over the Amblève in their field of fire. (*Jacobs Bibliothèque de Stavelot*)

running, disregarding any noise we might make, and when we got a good distance away, we took cover.

KA-BOOM! It was a terrific explosion. The stone masonry houses near the bridge collapsed and any remaining windows were all blown out. It must have been a shock to the Boche. Our artillery stopped firing and we were all stood on the sidewalk unharmed when at least one Jerry machine gun started firing in our direction. We quickly took cover by going into the houses through the windows and doors, and after a few minutes the firing stopped. Fortunately, no one was hurt. When relative calm was restored, I needed to see if our action had been successful. Sergeant Richardson accompanied me and, as

The 743rd Tank Battalion and infantrymen of the 30th ID held Stavelot firmly. (*NARA*)

> *discreetly as possible, we approached the structure. The first span had disappeared; mission accomplished. When asked by press correspondent Hal Boyle about our action, our company commander, Captain James Rice said, "No German tank can jump that". After the bridge was demolished, our company fought alongside the 117th IR until January 1945.*[20]

The two Tigers saw none of this and were instead used as support to protect the flanks of KG Knittel at both ends of the Stavelot-Trois-Ponts road. Wendt's Tiger 133 blocked the approaches towards Stavelot, while Brandt's 132 did the same on the other side. The day of the 19th passed without any other notable event for the two heavy tanks. In the early morning, fighters from I. SS-Panzergrenadier Regiment 1 took the light bridge of the Petit Spay to cross the Amblève and join the tip of the Peiper column at La Gleize. Knittel had to regain the area around the destroyed bridge in order to re-establish his lines of communication. Although they could make a difference against the GIs entrenched in the houses on the edge of the town, it seems that the two Tiger IIs remained in the rear, as their crews were very wary of the soldiers armed with bazookas. Their attitude is understandable, because if the 150 mm of front armour was safe from hollow charge rockets, this was not the case for the engine bay, which was much thinner, and a rocket fired from a first floor window could cause significant damage.

Finally, the assault failed in the face of American resistance. In the afternoon of 20 December, the 505th Parachute Infantry Regiment, 82nd Airborne Division, quickly joined by Task Force *Lovelady*, cut off Peiper's rear at Trois-Ponts. The American tankers continued towards Stavelot and came face to face with Brandt's tank. Four Sherman

In the afternoon, the 505th Parachute Infantry Regiment, 82nd Airborne Division, quickly joined by Task Force *Lovelady*, cut Peiper's rear at Trois-Ponts. (*NARA*)

tanks were destroyed, blocking the GIs' attempts. Notwithstanding this meagre victory, the two Tigers were locked in a trap on the N33 between Trois-Ponts and Stavelot, bordered on one side by the Amblève River and on the other by a steep wooded slope impassable for the two beasts. While Tiger 132 faced Trois-Ponts, from where it hit a Sherman, Wendt's 133 was sent to support the SS towards Stavelot.[21] In his testimony, Wendt stated:

> *Early in the morning of 21 December, the light bridge at Petit Spay collapsed under the weight of a Jagdpanzer. During the night of 21 to 22 December, the engineers were called*

A Panzerjäger IV L/70 ventured onto the bridge over the Petit Spay and crushed it under its weight. It is seen here lying in the Amblève. (*Jacobs Bibliothèque de Stavelot*)

> *in to rebuild the bridge. On the morning of 22 December, the pioneer engineers began to build a temporary bridge under heavy artillery and mortar fire. Casualties were high among the engineering unit. A metal girder about 40 centimetres wide was laid across the Amblève but a second one could not be put in place because of the high water. Due to the heavy losses, but also because of the extreme gravity of the general situation in the area, it was decided not to continue with the construction of the bridge.*[22]

The following day, the Americans increased their pressure from Stavelot. The Waffen-SS had no choice but to retreat, one section was even surrounded. Knowing that his men were encircled, Knittel sent Wendt's Tiger 133 towards Stavelot to rescue the besieged men. Arriving at the western edge of Stavelot, the Tiger was hit by numerous Sherman shells, but none had any effect; the US tanks could not position themselves to take it by

The German Pioneers tried to build a new bridge, but it could not be completed due to the US artillery shelling. (*NARA*)

the flanks as the configuration of the terrain did not allow it. During this exchange of fire, Wendt's Tiger managed to damage two US tanks. He explains what happened:

On 22 December, I was ordered by Sturmbannführer Knittel to free the trapped comrades on the western edge of Stavelot. They were in the cellar of a building and occupied the ground floor, each trying to hit the other with hand grenades. Knittel described the house to me exactly. I took my tank to force the enemy out of the building. After a while I could not see anything in the dense fog and returned to the command post. I reported to Sturmbannführer Knittel, who put the telephone in my hand and said: "Talk to those people yourself!" There was still a telephone line with our isolated soldiers, although the situation in the house had not changed at all.

I set off once more for Stavelot. I wanted to do my best. Fifty metres before the entrance to the town, after a loud explosion nearby in the tumult of the battle, our tank suddenly turned around. The intercom system was no longer working. My driver drove us to the

Wendt's Tiger 133 withdrew hastily and ended up in a ditch. It was found there by the Americans despite the Germans' attempts to sabotage it with explosives. (*Rights reserved*)

> *command post at full speed and headed for Petit Spay, where about 100 metres before the bridge we landed in a ditch. It was then for the first time I realised the reasons for my driver's abrupt U-turn. We had been hit on the rolling ring of the tank turret, where it is inserted into the gunner's compartment. The armour in this area is about 5 centimetres thick. The shell had impacted downwards and penetrated the post. The driver's access hatch was torn off, the radio was dead and shrapnel had damaged the transmission, automatic steering and hydraulic gear change. As a result of the loss of oil and the drop in oil pressure, the tank became unmanageable. It was completely immobilised in the ditch, but we could still fire.*[23]

In a Tiger, as in all German tanks from the Panzer III onwards, the body gunner was in charge of the radio and the internal communication system. The equipment was placed on his right. The American anti-tank shell destroyed this part of the machine, killing the operator and disabling the intercom. This explains why Wendt could no longer communicate with his driver. The latter took the initiative to withdraw after they had been hit, without being able to explain to his boss what was really going on. The transmission system of such a heavy tank was operated by a hydraulic system and the impact of the American shell had caused an oil leak. The pressure in the pipes had dropped rapidly and so the tank had become impossible to steer, thus ending up in a ditch.

Furthermore, it seems that Wendt did not place the action on the right day. The diary of the S3 of the 743rd Tank Battalion places the Tiger attack two days earlier. It states: '*Three tanks of the 3rd Platoon, B15, 16 and 18 came up the street to support friendly infantry. A Mark VI*[24] *appeared on a street corner 50 yards away. A tank destroyer fired a shell and moved to safety. The B15 fired three Armour Piercings which bounced off the enemy tank. The*

The Sherman had very little chance of victory against the Tiger. At Stavelot, a Sherman manages to damage Tiger 133 – but only after four attempts. (*NARA*)

Photo of the Petit Spay in spring 1945. The German wrecks show the harshness of the raids in this area. (*Jacobs Bibliothèque de Stavelot*)

B15 fired a smoke shell and took cover behind the corner.'[25] The report states that the German machine was not destroyed. Therefore, there is no claim of its destruction.

On Sunday, 24 December, the matter was finally settled. Kampfgruppe Knittel, exhausted and out of ammunition, had to withdraw to the other side of the river. The decision was all the more justified as it was useless to maintain efforts on the right bank of the Amblève following Peiper's withdrawal. German pioneers had placed a footbridge across the river, allowing the SS to cross with dry feet. About fifty vehicles remained, these having escaped the artillery and the Allied air force. At the Petit Spay bridge, the

Another view of the Petit Spay. The building visible on the hill in the background is where Jürgend Brandt died of his wounds. (*Jacobs Bibliothèque de Stavelot*)

air was unbreathable and any movement was detected by the US artillery observers, who were very efficient. Tiger 132, the only one still operational, in which SS-Oberscharführer Jürgen Brandt was mounted, remained ambushed at the Petit Spay bridge and kept the Americans at bay. Meanwhile, the order to evacuate was given.

Although the banks at the bridge sloped gently, the depth of the river, swollen by the winter rains, did not allow the surviving Tiger 132 to pass, nor would the American artillery allow it to cross to the other bank. Cap's Panzer (short for 'Captain', Jürgen Brandt's nickname), slowly made its way to Antoine's Farm to protect its damaged track. Arriving at Kampfgruppe HQ, Brandt was told that it was possible to cross the river. Although the ford was not indicated on contemporary maps, there was indeed a passage formerly used to cross the Amblève, at the 'passage des charrettes', a place known to the local inhabitants.[26] On the night of 23/24 December the thermometer fell to -7°C. The ground had firmed up, making it easier for the vehicles to move through the meadows bordering the river. Tiger 132 left the road and headed towards the banks of the Amblève, with the survivors of Tiger 133 on board. The low point by the river, known as 'The Seven Mountains', was invisible to artillery observers, which explains why the transit of German forces via the ford was protected from the avalanche of shells that Uncle Sam was not shy in launching.

Wendt explains how his Ardennes adventure ended:

Early in the morning of 25 December I was summoned to Sturmbannführer Knittel, who informed me that we had to be on the other side of the Amblève by 0900hrs. There were no other orders apart from that. SS-Mann Noss was given the task of passing on the orders

Two pictures of the turret of Tiger 133, taken from different angles. Wendt's charges did not work and it is therefore possible that the turret was blown by US engineers. (*Jacobs Bibliothèque de Stavelot*)

The turret was blown off before the tank was moved to the banks of the Amblève. (*Jacobs Bibliothèque de Stavelot*)

to Tank 132. As Noss arrived, Oberscharführer Jürgen Brandt got out of his tank and at that moment a shell burst. Brandt and Noss were killed instantly. This was the only shell that fell in the vicinity. Unterscharführer Otterbein took the rest of the crew to the other side of the river and then to the top of the hill where there was a lonely house with a command post. Only my driver and I remained living in our tank, 133. The machine gun operator had been killed on 24 December. At 0900hrs we placed an explosive charge in the gun barrel and one in the engine compartment and lit them. Then we crawled up to the footbridge that was still in place, the remains of the work the engineers had built, and crossed the water to the other side of the Amblève. We did not hear any explosion from the tank, not even later, when we were able to observe our tank for over an hour. The next day we reported to the company. The first company gave what tanks they had left to the second and third companies and we headed back to Germany. On 31 December 1944, at 1800hrs, we were back where we started from, in Oerlingen in the Teutoburg Forest.[27]

In reality, Brandt's shrapnel-ridden body was taken to the farm that served as a dispensary, where he died two hours later. The Mignon Farm, later destroyed after the war, was situated halfway between the Antoine Farm and the Petit Spay bridge. After taking the platoon leader to the field hospital, the survivors of Tiger 132 returned to the cart track and crossed the Amblève in their tanks to join their lines at Wanne.

From a defensive point of view, the presence of the two Tigers allowed Knittel to resist the American armoured thrusts for nearly four days. On the other hand, their offensive effectiveness was hampered by their lack of manoeuvrability in urban areas. Too large, with armour designed to confront the enemy at long range and neglecting the upper horizontal parts, they were unable to break through the Stavelot lock. Consequently, their enormous size was disadvantageous as they tried to cross the town.

Tiger 008: Victim of Transmission

Tiger 008, belonging to the battalion's adjutant SS-Untersturmführer Eduard Kalinowsky, the battalion's second in command, suffered from mechanical problems with either the engine or the clutch. It passed through the town immediately after Peiper's Panthers, before the route was blocked, forcing the crew to stop at the Antoine Farm. While waiting for a repair company that never came, the men stayed at the farm, where Knittel later met them. The tank was ordered to serve as a bunker and to position itself in such a way as to be able to resist a potential US attack coming from Stavelot. The tank crew carried out their mission and held the Americans who were trying to leave Stavelot at bay, until the encircled German troops in the pocket were able to escape from what was beginning to look an awful lot like a cauldron. Before abandoning it at the time of the evacuation, the crew sabotaged its machine by emptying the recoil brake of hydraulic fluid, meaning the last shell it fired finally rendered the gun unusable.

Tiger 008 was photographed as it passed through the village of Tondorf. (*NARA*)

Tiger 008 seen from the front. (*Rights reserved*)

Tiger 008 was immobilised due to a transmission failure. (*Janco*)

After clearing the pocket at Petit Spay, the 117th IR moved towards its new target. (*NARA*)

Motorbikes were used to reconnoitre the route ahead of the heavy tanks. (*NARA*)

Tiger 222: Dead in a Duel at the Water's Edge

The Stavelot bridge was the key to victory for both sides. In the early morning of 19 December, the bridge was the No Man's Land between the belligerents. It came under fire from two M10 Tank Destroyers of C Company, 823rd Tank Destroyer Battalion (TD Bat.), who were entrenched 100 metres away. This was a very good position for them as from there they could engage the Tigers by attacking them from the side. Based on the ballistic tables available for this ammunition, the theoretical maximum distance at which the flank of an 80 mm Tiger II, inclined at 25°, could be pierced is a maximum of 2,078 metres. At this range, the armour-piercing head still theoretically has a speed of 615 m/s. On the other hand, the same graphs show that the frontal protection of the German heavyweights was total, even at close range. The 117th Infantry Regiment's war diary states that at 1307hrs, a column of tanks attacked the bridge from the south. SS-Oberscharführer Kurt Sowa's Tiger 222 was in the lead, but did not reach the bridge. Captain Tom Raney witnessed the scene:

> *Mac and I were on the second floor of a building under observation. From a window we could see the River Amblève and the bridge leading into Stavelot from the south, about 135 metres away. From the window on our left we could see one of Mac's M10s, commanded, I believe, by Sergeant Ray Dudley, which covered the bridge and the road leading to it from the south-east. This road, which runs down the hillside from the Amblève, was lined with buildings, except for the last few yards before the bridge. We saw the long cannon of the Tiger emerging from behind the last house. The M10 gunner must have followed the tank in his telescopic sight and, as the Tiger left the cover of the building, he fired an*

Tiger 222 was the only one to pass through the Kaiserbarrack. (*NARA*)

> *armour-piercing shot which penetrated the armour on the right side, above the tracks, about 35 cm below the turret and 12 cm behind the hull. The Tiger stopped and, strangely, did not catch fire.*

According to other sources, the crew evacuated the tank; a version confirmed by Captain Leland Cofer:

> *While at my post in the upstairs window of the house, I witnessed a duel between one of our M10 Tank Destroyers and a Kraut tank on the other side of the river. After pretending to cross the bridge, the German tank reversed and crashed through a fence. The Tank Destroyer fired a couple of shells into the side of the enemy tank. Seconds later a smoke grenade was thrown out of the Panzer's hatch, and one by one the five crew members fled into the nearby building.*[28]

As explained above, in the evening the captain fulfilled his mission and destroyed the bridge. This brilliant action marked the beginning of the end for the Kampfgruppe. Now cut in two and almost out of fuel, the bulk of its armoured strike force, estimated at twenty-seven Tigers, remained on the wrong side of the Amblève. Of no use following

The M10 (left) and M36 (right) were used by the Tank Destroyer Battalion against the tanks of KG Peiper. (*NARA*)

Tiger 222, destroyed at Stavelot, was the last tank of the schwere SS-Panzer-Abteilung 501 to reach the outskirts of the town. (*Jacobs Bibliothèque de Stavelot*)

the evacuation of the La Gleize cauldron, it was redirected to the Bastogne sector a few days later.

The photographs of the destroyed Tiger 222 show three hits on the right flank, two on the lower edge and another in the middle, about 30 centimetres under the turret and about 10 centimetres behind the front turret armour. It was probably this latter hit that was the fatal one. The Tiger suffered an oblique hit and it is likely that the perforating bullet passed through the cockpit and ended up in the left-hand part of the engine compartment. This shock explains why the vehicle stopped immediately.

The Gepanzerte Kampfgruppe was led by Obersturmbannführer Peiper. (*NARA*)

Tiger 222 was at the head of the column which tried to retake the Amblève. Two M10s had taken position at the foot of Stavelot Abbey (the large white building in the background). (*Jacobs Bibliothèque de Stavelot*)

The distance between the two tanks was 140 metres, which means the projectile perforated the side of the tank without any problem. At least one shell hit when the Tiger was backing up. Witnesses state that the shell entered under the turret. An analysis of the internal workings of the Panzer VI allows us to understand the nature of the damage caused.

The turret number 222 can be seen in this picture. (*Jacobs Bibliothèque de Stavelot*)

If the projectile entered the engine compartment, the dozens of red-hot shards would inevitably set the behemoth on fire. However, witnesses say that this was not the case, so a shell entering in a highly flammable area is unlikely. The combat cell of the tank was occupied by three men: the tank commander, the loader and the gunner. Again, if white-hot metal shrapnel entered the combat compartment, there would be at least one serious casualty, while all the crew members might escape under cover of a smoke flare.

At the same time, the armour-piercing shell did not enter in such a way as to neutralise the tank gunners. The tank was at the beginning of its engagement, meaning the shell racks were full. It is easy to imagine the terrifying effect a hit on the ammunition store would be: the Panzer would literally explode. This means the most likely theory is that the shot came from underneath the combat cell, underneath which were the batteries, the hydraulic pump connected to the drive shaft which controlled the clutch, the gearbox and the turret.

Tiger 222 did not catch fire. Rather, its crew threw a smoke grenade and took refuge in the building in the background. (*Jacobs Bibliothèque de Stavelot*)

The right side of the machine was hit by three shells. (*Rights reserved*)

If the hydraulic pump had been hit, the gun would probably have collapsed, which was not the case. Therefore, batteries releasing toxic gases and/or a broken driveshaft were most likely responsible for Tiger 222 being abandoned under heavy fire.

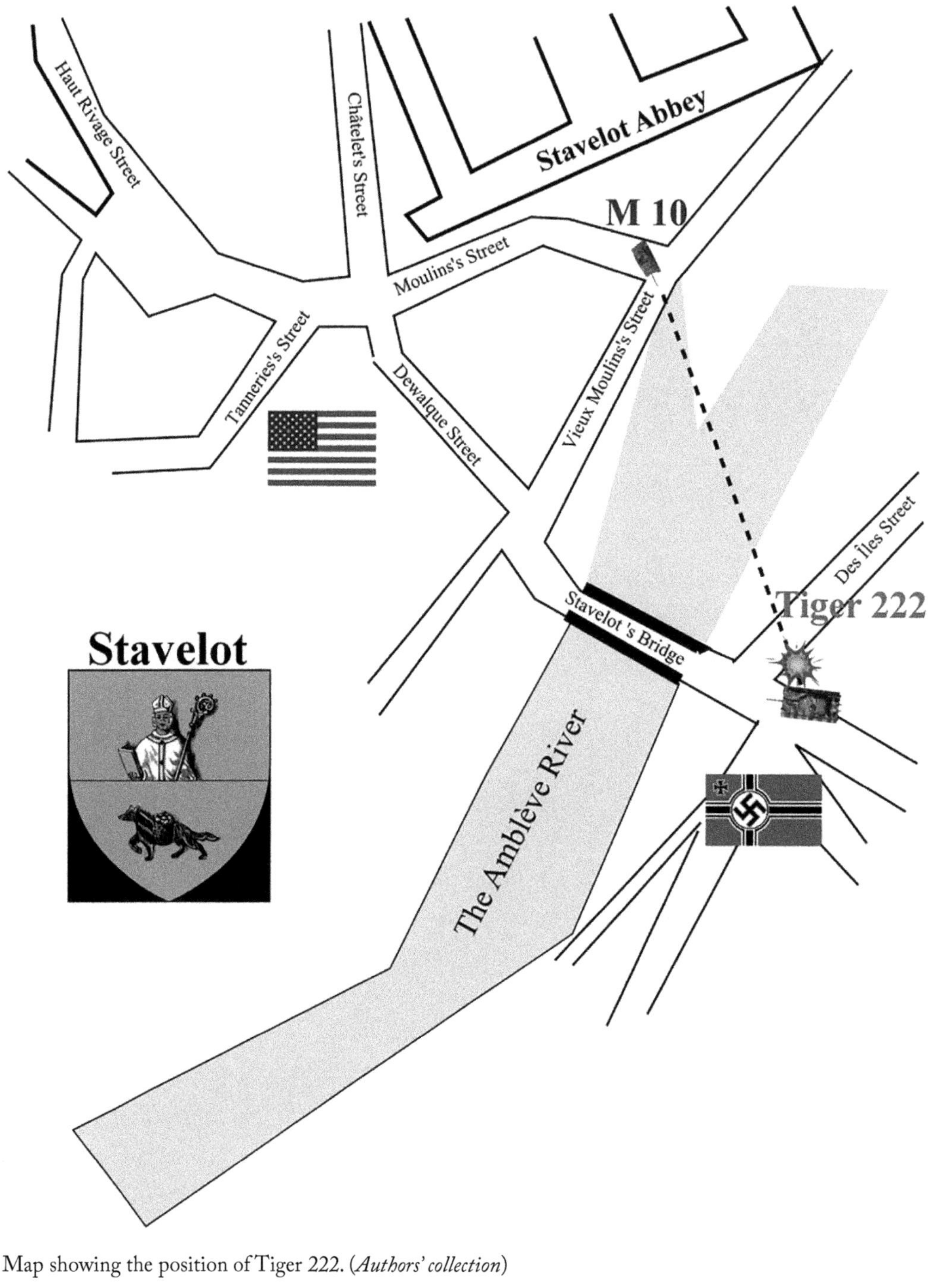

Map showing the position of Tiger 222. (*Authors' collection*)

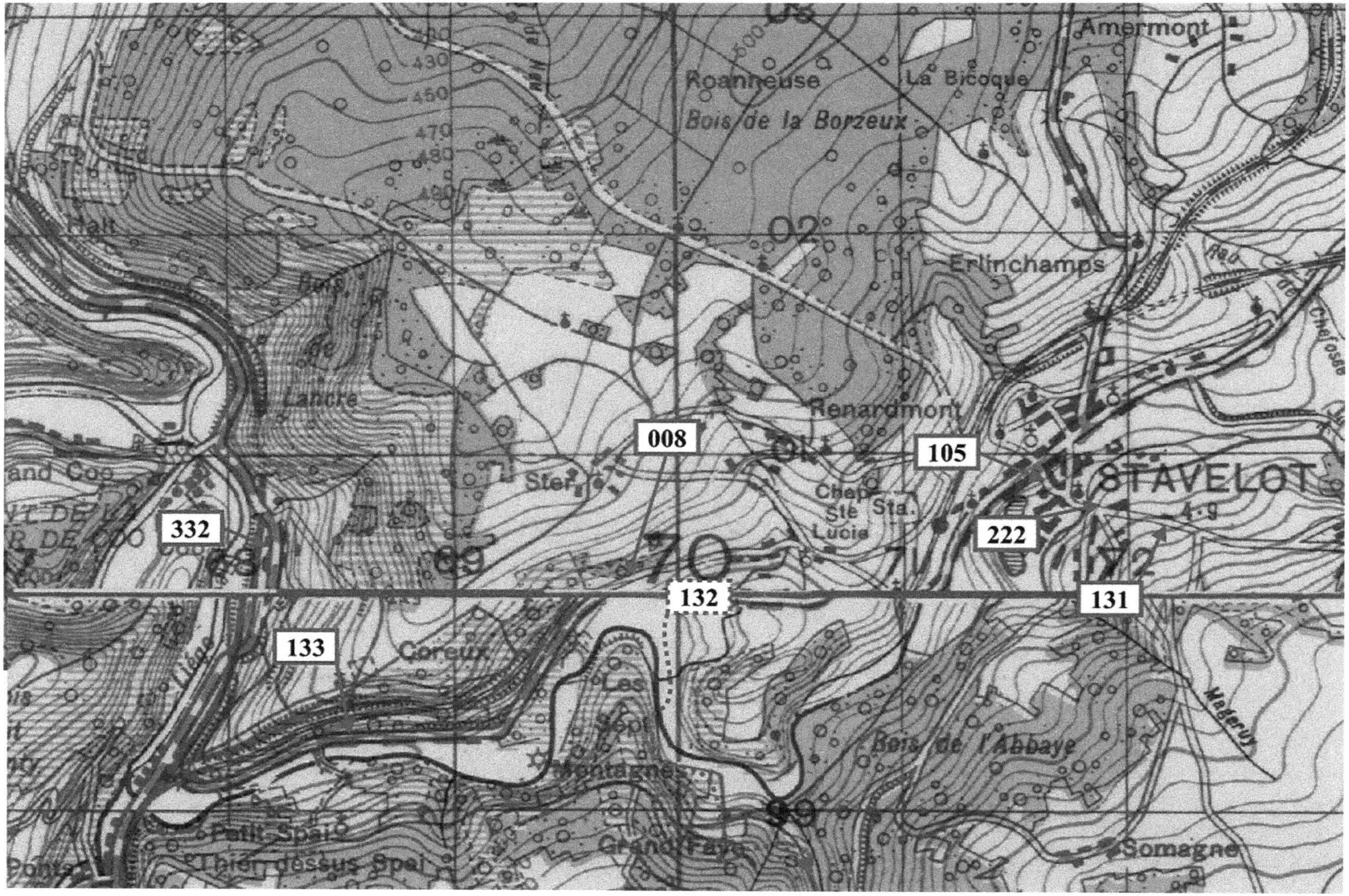

Stavelot. (*Authors' collection*)

Chapter 4

From Trois-Ponts to La Gleize

Tiger 332: The Unpredictable One

SS-Unterscharführer Otto Blase's 332 engine was found intact in Biester (Coo). Its tanks were empty, having run out of fuel at the end of the day on 18 December before reaching La Gleize. Two very young SS men under the age of 18 were left in charge of the machine

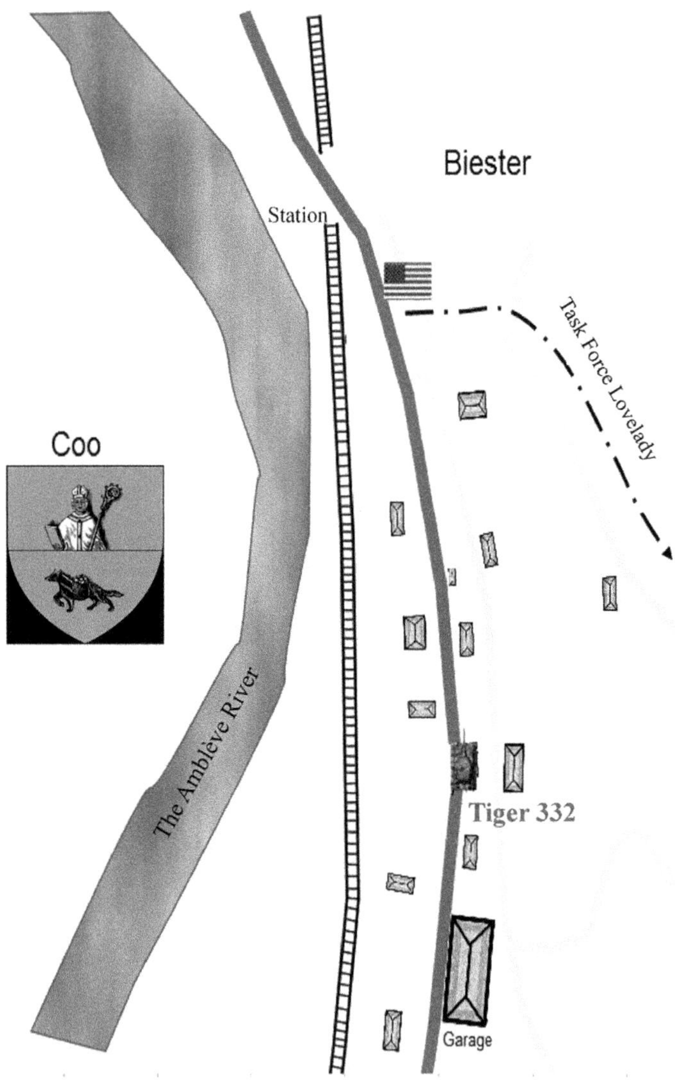

Map showing the position of Tiger 332. (*Authors' collection*)

Tiger 332 was evacuated to Aberdeen, Maryland. (*NARA*)

and taken prisoner, without resistance, by the men of Task Force *Lovelady*. The tank was parked on the left side of the road, near the front of Charles Collinet's house. Seeing the motionless monster, the lead Sherman of Task Force *Lovelady* fired an incendiary shell, which also set fire to the house.[1] The Collinet house would be never rebuilt, and its ruins are still visible today. The 332 would later be recovered by the American 463rd Ordnance Evacuation Company to be examined at Aberdeen Proving Ground, Maryland, after an incredible odyssey.

Tiger 223: The Giant with Feet of Clay

On its way from Tondorf, SS-Unterscharführer Walter Müller's Tiger had already covered about 80 kilometres. This distance, especially after crossing over the Stavelot bridge, which had already forced Tiger 132 to stop, was too much for the engine, and the vehicle derailed while negotiating a bend in front of La Gleize. It was abandoned by its crew while waiting for a repair company that never came. On 20 December, it was reported by the men of the 105th Engineer Company and on the 24th, was targeted by a 90-mm anti-aircraft gun. Meanwhile, the GIs of the 117th Infantry Regiment threw grenades inside to put it out of action for good.[2]

Tiger 223 was almost at La Gleize when its right track broke while turning. Note that the GI in the centre is armed with a Sturmgewehr 44. (*NARA*)

Only five Tigers arrived at La Gleize at around 1300hrs on 18 December: 104, 204, 221, 213 and 334. They continued on towards Cheneux and Rahier, needing to find a way across the River Lienne. At 1330hrs they came under an aerial attack, but no damage was caused. Throughout the evening, reconnaissance elements were busy trying to find a bridge. However, the US sappers had done their job very well and the Germans abandoned their search around midnight, with the machines heading back to the small village.

Tiger 104: The Sacrificial Martyr

The night ride was fatal for Tiger 104, which broke a track. The lack of fuel was beginning to be felt; its tank was drained and it would not move again. After the evacuation of the village, it was later found by the GIs who would use it for target practice for their bazookas in a small, narrow street in the village. Tiger 104 was unusual in that it did not have a turret number, just 'Balkan Kreuz' written on its side.

After resting at Remouchamp, paratroopers of 504th PIR return to La Gleize for bazooka training on the abandoned Tiger 104. (*NARA*)

Gathering around the martyred target. (*NARA*)

This picture shows why Tiger 104 was lost: its caterpillar track broke on the way back from Cheneux. (*NARA*)

Tigers 221 and 213

The small village of La Gleize occupies a promontory overlooking the entire valley. While Peiper tried to find a passage to the west, he ordered von Westernhagen to deploy his Tiger hedgehogs to defend the eastern approaches to the village.[3] The SS-Sturmbannführer took advantage of the excellent range of the 88-mm gun to close off the entire valley, as they were able to destroy any Shermans that dared to venture too near.

Tiger 221 took part in a blocking mission on the road to Roanne, in order to keep the escape route open in the direction of Trois-Ponts, by the Maréchal windmill. In addition to the Panzer VI, the Sperrgruppe 'Mühle'[4] was composed of a Panzer IV, an Sd.Kfz. 234/3 Puma equipped with a 7.5-cm short gun and a platoon of 'tank breakers'. Each took up positions on either side of the road to be defended, at the exit of a bend in the hillside. If the location was ideal for an ambush, it was imperative that the Germans were able to hold it, because if they failed, the retreat road would come under fire. SS-Hauptscharführer Nüske was sent to reconnoitre and discovered a column of thirty US vehicles on the way to the mill. Back in the group, he proposed the following plan of attack:

A Panzer IV Ausf H/J similar to these seen here accompanied Sperrgruppe Mühle. (*NARA*)

An Sd Kfz 234/3 with a 75-mm gun for close support accompanied Tiger 221 to the Marechal Mill. (*NAC*)

Shermans arrive to counter KG Peiper. (*NARA*)

Tiger 221 was found heavily damaged near the Wérimont Farm. (*Rights reserved*)

> *Our Panzer IV is to the left of the mill, the Tiger on the right. When a sufficient number of American machines are in the open, the Panzer VI will destroy the lead one and we the last. Then we can clear the column from the back to the middle. The 'Friends' will not be able to deploy, as the road is too narrow there. We have the element of surprise and the terrain advantage. If things go wrong, we can fall back into the valley.*[5]

However, the Panzerführer in the heavy tank rejected the plan: *'Fire up the hill! I'm not going to kill myself; I only have 3 cm of armour on the roof.'* In reality, 4 not 3 centimetres of steel protected the horizontal upper parts of the Tiger II, although this does not really change the tank commander's reasoning. However, the discussion highlights one of the weaknesses of the tank's armour, which limited its medium-range obstruction capabilities on steep slopes. In the end, the engagement did not take place as a broken track on the enemy's side caused the column to stop for the night. The next day, the Sperrgruppe was back in the lines.

Tigers 221 and 213 took up position in a field at the Wérimont Farm. From there, the two machines threatened the whole Roanne–Coo road. In broad daylight, they hindered the progress of Combat Command B, 3rd Armored Division, and about fifteen Shermans of the 743rd Tank Battalion on their way to Trois-Ponts. Over the following days they would be targeted by American artillery, which eventually put them out of

Tiger 213 was abandoned in the same area as Tiger 221. (*Rights reserved*)

Tiger 213 was found with its gun blown up. It would be replaced by a 75-mm gun. (*Janco*)

The Belgian army later returned to where the fighting had taken place. Tiger 213 is still at La Gleize, today. (*Authors' collection*)

action. No. 213, which still stands in the village of La Gleize, had the end of its barrel cut in two to serve as a gutter in a farmhouse for years... This part of the tank, as well as the muzzle brake, were recovered when the vehicle was renovated. Meanwhile, Tiger 221's electrical firing system eventually failed. It's commander, Hantusch, was wounded in the head and took refuge in a farm cellar.

There are many books on the fate of the Peiper Tigers. Although they have been very useful in helping to retrace the twists and turns of history, in the end we have only worked with primary sources: period photographs, eyewitness testimonies, interviews and combat reports. For a long time we hesitated about the exact numbers of two of the six tanks lost at La Gleize: 221 and 223. However, a photograph allowed us to be sure that Tiger 223 was indeed the tank lost at the foot of the hill.

For Tiger 221, the investigation was more complicated. Indeed, Tiger 211 is mentioned in some writings, with Hantusch listed as its commander. There are no pictures of the wreckage available that allow us to identify with confidence whether it is 221 or 211. Confirmation of its identification was finally provided through the testimony of the eyewitness, Mr Gregoire. Aged 17 at the time, he returned to La Gleize on 9 January 1945. His house, like so many others, had been badly damaged by the war. The young man immediately became fascinated with the history of the fighting in his local area. He visited every wreck and witnessed the destruction and evacuation of the damaged vehicles by the American engineers and a Liège scrap metal company between July and November 1945. When we contacted him, he was clear: 223 was indeed at the bottom of the village and 221 was with 213 in the field by the Wérimont Farm.

Tiger 334: Last Stand

On 22 December, the pressure from Borgoumont increased. This was the only approach road overlooking La Gleize and it posed the greatest threat to the entrenched camp. Around 1300hrs, Peiper ordered an attack to retake the hamlet. The assault was led by a Sherman, two Panzer IVs and Tiger 334.

Serge Fontaine, an eyewitness to the event, explains what happened:

> *The Panzer column, preceded by a Sherman, was spotted from Roanne, before entering the place known as Les Tchéoux, and was caught under heavy artillery fire. The Sherman exploded under the weight of the shells in the middle of the road... The other crews tried*

Tiger 334 was destroyed at Bourgoumont after its right track took a direct hit. The Sherman in the ditch was used by the Germans. (*NARA*)

to clear the road with cables, but it was impossible due to the intense shelling. The track of another tank broke in front of the hotel in Tscheous, and the vehicle slid sideways, unrolling its thick steel ribbon. Gradually they fell back, losing a third tank 200 metres from the Nabonruy bridge.[6]

The 117th Infantry Regiment's logbook confirms the account: '*1310hrs: 300 infantry and four tanks advanced on Borgoumont towards the north-east. At 1415hrs a tiger tank was reported (6618-0386) near Roanne. At 1420hrs the above message was given to the artillery and S3 requested to shell these coordinates. At 1440hrs three men evacuated the tank and it was stopped.*'[7]

However, the destruction of the Tiger cannot be confirmed using these two sources. The photograph of the machine found after the battle shows that the track is still in place and suggests a frontal blow to the track in the right sprocket.

The account of First Lieutenant Joseph A. Couri, serving with A Company, 2nd Platoon, 743rd Tank Battalion tells us more:

The next day my platoon and Lieutenant Jenkins' 3rd Platoon were alerted to move to La Gleize with K Coy of the III/117th Infantry Regiment. From the Infantry CP I was called back to the hill north of Bourgoumont. This hill overlooked the whole valley and from

The 743rd Tank Battalion supported the infantry of the 30th ID. (*NARA*)

The infantry took up position on the high ground. (*NARA*)

> *there we had a view of the road to La Gleize. From above the command post the infantry captain was watching the German tanks and infantry through his binoculars. They were at the right distance to be hit by my platoon. I immediately made contact by radio with Sergeant Jones, who was in position near the bend and could not see the approaching German tanks. I signalled him when they entered the bend and as the German tanks came into his line of fire, he fired his gun. The first shot ricocheted off the front of the Tiger tank. The sergeant said to me over the radio in amazement, "Did you see that?" "Yes!" I said, when suddenly the German tank, after backing up a little on the road, started firing wildly with its big gun. After a few minutes it moved forward again. I warned Jones of the manoeuvre and the same thing happened again when the sergeant fired another shot at the front of the tank; the shell bounced back as well. Same result on the third attempt. But the fourth shot hit one of the tracks and, with a demolished track, the tank backed up quickly and soon ran aground in the ditch. The tank was abandoned and the German column withdrew towards La Gleize. Later, a 90-mm gun was installed on the east side of the hill and, with a few shells, it set the tank on fire.*[8]

This account is very accurate and is confirmed by the after action report of the 743rd TB, which states: '*Enemy infantry also came under fire 400 yards south west of Bourgoumont. A call for artillery put one tank out of action. Sergeant Robert C. Jones destroyed a Mark VI in this action.*'[9] The battle report perfectly completes the information given by the two eyewitnesses. Better still, it reconciles them. The artillery destroyed the Sherman and a

Jones' Sherman fire was directed by his lieutenant, who was watching the Tiger's movements. (*NARA*)

face-to-face battle between the armoured vehicles defeated Tiger 334. What gave the Sherman victory in this engagement was the remote assistance of Lieutenant Couri, who allowed Jones to come out of hiding, fire and withdraw to cover. On the fourth attempt, a hit in the caterpillar track immobilised the tank, which was then finished off with 90-mm anti-aircraft fire.

Photographs of the Tiger taken after the fighting do not contradict these additional versions. It should also be added that the machine was then used to test the effect of anti-tank mines on caterpillar tracks.

This photograph, taken after the war, leaves no doubt about the number of the Tiger lost at Bourgoumont. (*Rights reserved*)

Tiger 204

On the night of 17/18 December, due to mechanical problems with Tiger 205, Company Commander Rolf Mobius climbed into Eduard Stadler's 204. SS-Hauptsturmführer Rolf Mobius was an ace of the armoured division and is credited with 127 enemy tanks destroyed. Back from Neufmoulin, following Peiper's orders the Tiger IIs had to protect the Kampfgruppe's rear by mounting an ambush at La Gleize.

Rudolf Mobius, Rolf to his friends and family, hid himself in the centre of the village. On 19 December, a thick fog hung over the region, but at about 1500hrs, a break in the fog appeared. Four Shermans from A Company, 743rd Tank Battalion, came down towards the valley, from Roanne. On the way they saw Tiger 223 immobilised by the loss of its caterpillar track 1.3 kilometres from the village of La Gleize. Uncle Sam's tanks targeted it with their shells, whose red glow made it possible to follow their trajectory, hitting the monster hard. There was no retaliation and so the tanks moved upwards to have a better angle of fire.

A Sherman, however, stopped in the meadow just above Abel Fontaine's farm. The local inhabitants watched, quite unwisely, as the situation developed. From the tank emerged two crew members: the tank commander, Sergeant Goodrige and the gunner. Tiger 204 had just spotted its target, so the firing procedure was initiated. The sighting system of the Tiger was based on the mathematical principle of Thales' theorem; small triangles in the reticle corresponded to an angle opening of 1/16. Through the reticle,

A Sherman M4 (75) of the 743rd Tank Battalion, destroyed by Tiger 204 (in which the company commander Mobius was riding) pictured after the war. (*Janco*)

Tiger 204 was found near Peiper's last command post at La Gleize. (*NARA*)

The 463rd Ordnance Evacuation Company was responsible for the repatriation of Tiger 204 to Aberdeen, Maryland. (*NARA*)

The Tiger's engine caught fire as a result of overheating. (*Rights reserved*)

at a distance of 500 metres, the base of the triangle was equivalent to 50 cm in width. At 1 kilometre, it was 1 metre. Gunners knew that the average tank was 6 metres long. So, if on the dial, the target tank occupied the width of six triangles, the distance to the target was 1,000 metres. If the tank was only three triangles wide, it was 2,000 metres away. The soldiers underwent constant training to memorise these rules of three so that it became automatic. The rise was then adjusted to match the distance to the target. The *Tiger Fibel*, the Tiger tank training manual, emphasised that the brightness affected the assessment of distances; the brighter the target, the closer it appeared.

Instructors logically stated that three estimates were better than one. In the tank, a well thought-out process was used to determine the firing parameters. When an enemy appeared on the horizon, the Panzerführer signalled this to his crew. The driver, who had an excellent field of vision, gave his assessment of the distance. The leader would average this with his own assessment, then the Richtschütze, who had a more accurate measuring system, gave his own. The commander once again calculated the average between his last calculation and that of his gunner. He increased it by 15 percent to take into account the height and gave the final firing coordinates. It was then up to the Panzerführer to determine the right ammunition to deal with the target. The Panzergranate 39 was ideal for destroying medium tanks up to a range of 2,000 metres. It was therefore probably this ammunition that was chosen. The orders would most likely proceed like this: '*Target at 01:00, range 2,000 m, panzergranate 39.*' At this range, it was a child's play, moreover, no Allied tank armour was able to withstand the terrible 88-mm gun. The gunner would reply: '*Target acquired*!', the loader: '*Gun loaded*!' '*Fire!*' The shell would leave the gun at a speed of 900 m/second. A few moments later, the projectile would pierce the armour of the US tank, explode immediately, and kill the three crew members remaining inside. The wreckage would then burn all night and Rolf would be able to paint an extra circle on the barrel of his tank to indicate another victory.

This easy victory would be the only one for Tiger 204. After the loss of Cheneux, which was taken over by paratroopers of the 82nd Airborne Division, and the capture of Stoumont by the GIs of the 30th Infantry Division, the German beast, like its comrades,

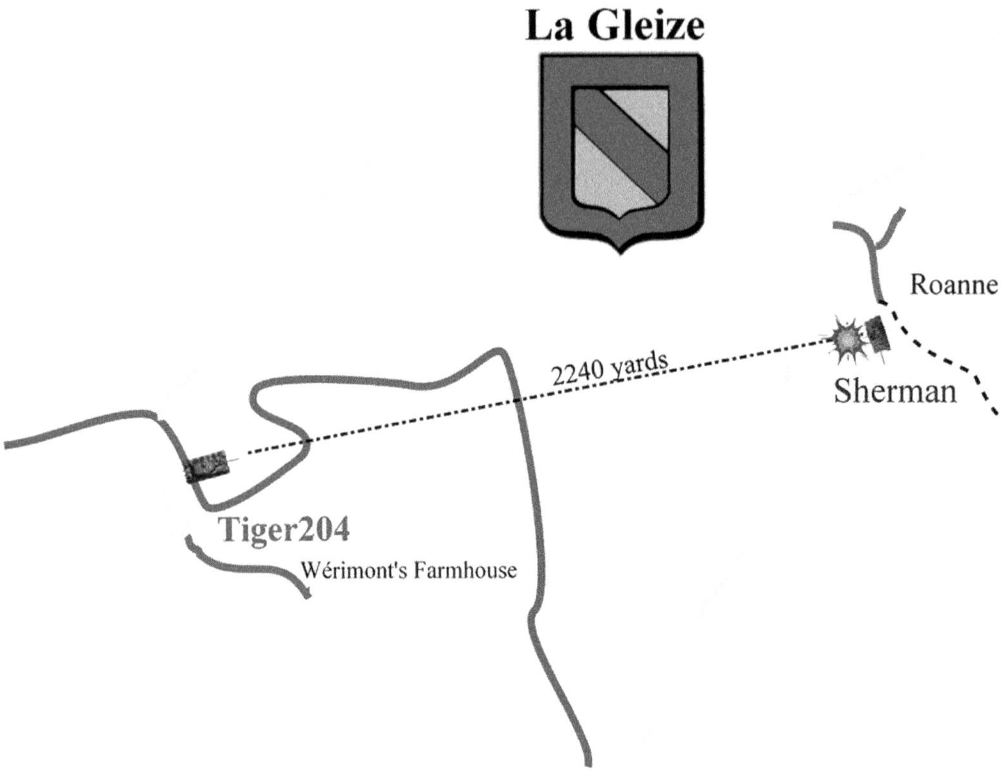

Map showing the position of Tiger 204. (*Authors' collection*)

The American mechanics turned the turret to the left to access the engine. (*NARA*)

found itself surrounded and out of fuel in La Gleize. The tank fell into the hands of the Americans, intact, and was later sent to the Aberdeen Proving Ground, Maryland. The 463rd Ordnance Evacuation Company was charged with repatriating the precious package. Petrol was poured into the tanks, and the vehicle started immediately. It was to be taken to Spa station, where it would be transported by rail to Antwerp. Given the weight of the Tiger II, however, the twelve-cylinder Maybach engine tended to overheat, and only experienced drivers were able to control it. The mechanics of the evacuation company were certainly not used to driving such heavy vehicles, and after 8.5 kilometres, near the hamlet of Neuville, travelling towards Francorchamps, the engine caught fire. The Tiger II was immobilized, and all attempts to restart its engine failed. The 204 was thus abandoned on the side of the road.

The reason for the overheating is easy to explain: the power unit was a "souped-up" version of the HL210. To give it more power, the German engineers enlarged the pistons by 130 mm. As a result, the cylinder head coolant had very little room to flow between the combustion chambers, which resulted in overheating. Furthermore, while V-engines had the advantage of being compact, they concentrated more power density than an inline or star configuration. More calories burned in a smaller space means that cooling was difficult, and in the case of the Tiger II, the matter became even more complicated,

Removing the filters. (NARA)

Tiger 204 was finally abandoned near the hamlet of Neuville, on the way to Francorchamps. (*NARA*)

Tiger 332 was loaded onto an American tank to reach Spa station. (*NARA*)

In theory, in order to be transported by rail, the Tiger's wide road tracks were usually replaced by transport tracks, which the 463rd Ordnance Evacuation Company did not have. (*Tegethoff*)

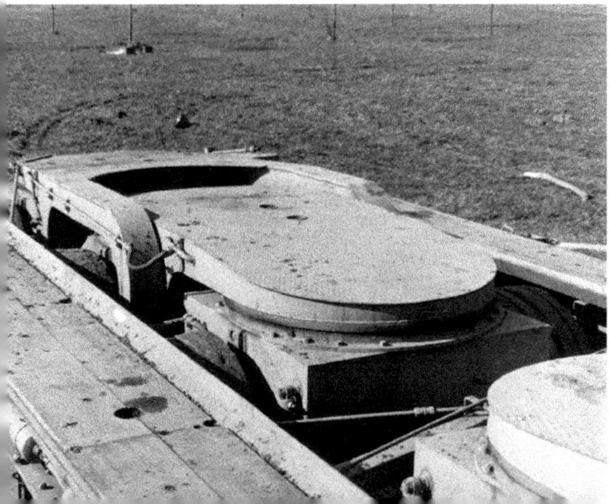

Tiger 332 was transported on a German trailer recovered from a field. The trailer was 23 tonnes when empty, and 11.87m long (16.15m with its ramps extended). The American report indicates that the wooden planks used to load the tank were new. Ironically, the trailer was used for the first time to repatriate a German heavy tank to the USA. (*NARA*)

413ORDE

413ORDE

Transported from Spa to Trooz, the Tiger was loaded onto the German trailer to be transported by road to the port of Antwerp, where it was then loaded onto a ship bound for the USA. (*NARA*)

as the power-to-weight ratio was 10 horsepower/ton. The engine was therefore stretched to the limit, making its weaknesses apparent.

Tiger 204 was driven by US mechanics who were not particularly familiar with this problem, and probably caused the engine to overheat by putting too much strain on it, especially as the roads in the area were very uneven. Abandoned on the side of the road, the tank was then pushed to the bottom of the valley where it stood for two years before being scrapped.

Finally, the Americans had to make do with the 332 that had run out of fuel on the Roanne–Coo road. It was a difficult recovery, as its tracks were stuck to the ground by the frost, meaning the recovery team of 463rd Ordnance Evacuation Company had to spread petrol on the ground before setting fire to it to free the undercarriage.

In order to avoid the problem of the engine overheating and the risk of the tank blocking the road again, an M9 trailer, designed to transport Shermans, was brought to the site. The average US tank 'only' weighed 40 tonnes, and as the Tiger II had a mass of 70 tonnes, the American platform loaded with the monster was put to a severe test. It was moved by two powerful Diamond M 19 trucks, one pulling ahead, the other pushing. The route chosen was Coo - La Gleize - Bergoumont and finally Spa station. Although equipped with twenty-four tyres (three axles of eight wheels, one at the front and two at

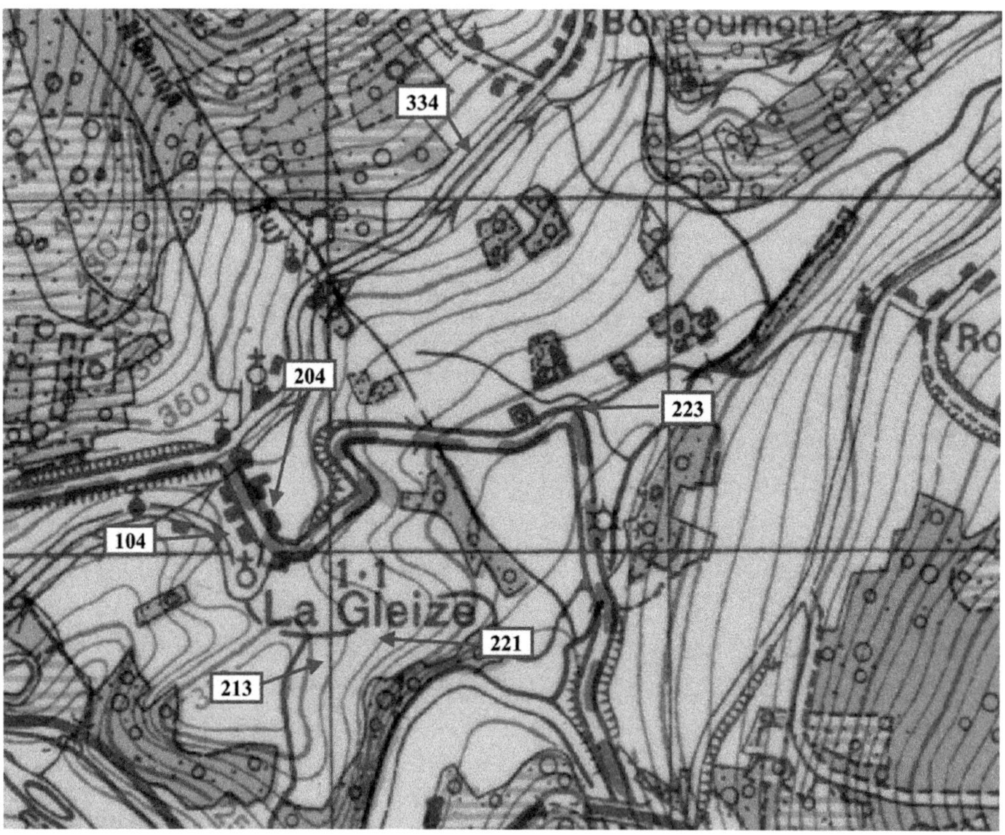

Lagleize. (*Authors' collection*)

the rear), the trailer was under pressure and some of the tyres caught fire due to the high temperatures. As there were no spare tyres, the convoy was forced to continue on the rims, at walking pace, to Spa station. The transport would take several days. Arriving at the station, a new disappointment awaited the men of the 463rd Ordonnance Evacuation Company: it was impossible to load the Tiger II onto the wagons. Indeed the combat-version of the Tiger II tank was equipped with 80-cm wide tracks, which had to be changed to narrower models when transported by train. In fact, it required the same tracks as the Panther, which were 66 cm wide. Due to the lack of available Panther tracks or a suitable trailer, Tiger 332 was thus to remain at Spa station until February 1945.

Meanwhile, in the First US Army sector, the Americans managed to recover a German trailer designed for heavy tank transport. We do not know how the vehicle managed to reach Trooz a few kilometres further on. However, it was in Trooz that it was loaded onto its special trailer and taken out of the area. The big beast was finally loaded and taken to the port of Antwerp, where it was sent to the US Army Tank Proving Ground. The 332 was only decommissioned in 1991 and was sent to the Patton Museum in Fort Knox, Kentucky, where it can still be admired today. For the purposes of the exhibition, the sides of the beast were opened to the public.

Tigers Decimated and Martyred

The Tiger IIs found in the Ardennes were subject to in-depth analysis by the ETO Technical Ordnance Intelligence, where the causes of destruction were analysed in depth. In the NARA archives, one also finds photographs taken after the fighting following tests on the effectiveness of the anti-tank mines. Unfortunately, it was not possible for these authors to determine which device it was. Nevertheless, the photographs are interesting for several reasons. Their existence shows that the American units wanted to ensure the capacity of their mines on the heaviest German machines. The result is clear: even if the Tiger did not really suffer, it was immobilised until the skids were replaced. The crews knew in theory how to repair this kind of damage, but it nevertheless forced them to lose a lot of time and left even more time for the enemy to take the initiative.

These Tigers from s. SS-Panzer-Abteilung 506 were lost north of Bastogne and are seen here being examined in detail. (*NARA*)

The units in the field conducted their own tests. Here the US anti-tank mine M1 tests the tracks of the Tiger II with some success. (*NARA*)

Chapter 5

Scattered in Small Detachments

After the evacuation of the La Gleize cauldron, the use of the schwere SS-Panzer-Abteilung 501 changed. The Tigers did not return to action immediately and were reassembled on 30 December, the battalion having lost only twelve of its forty-five tanks. The fact that the unit was at the end of the column prevented it from suffering greater losses, meaning there were still enough to equip two companies. 1. Kompanie left its remaining tanks in the Ardennes and returned to Oerlinghausen. The remaining tanks were requisitioned for the KG Möbius[1] and would not be used exclusively for 1. SS-Pz-Div, which had been in the Bastogne sector since 28 December.[2] The Tigers were to be engaged in various parts of the front, but even in the absence of available reports, it is possible to locate the unit by spotting the points in the battle where its elements were lost or highlighted in the American reports. Photographs of wrecks have been of great help in this investigation.

The I. SS-Panzer-Korps, to which the Tigers belonged, received the order to retake the defensive positions of 26. Volksgrenadier-Division by noon on January 1945.

Tiger 312: Goronne Defender

Another destroyed Tiger, Number 312, from the 501 was identified in the area of the fighting. In his excellent book, *Tiger in Combat*, Wolfgang Schneider states that the vehicle was lost near the Petit Spay bridge after being hit by a P38 bomb. Although its history is not linked directly with Peiper, we feel it is important to include its story here.

While Kampfgruppe Pieper was forced to abandon its vehicles, the 82nd Airborne Division held the banks of the Salm between Trois-Ponts and Vielsalm. The initial attack having failed, the 6. Panzer-Armee committed its II. SS-Panzer-Korps to bypassing the resistance zone from the south. Their orders were:

> *The 9. SS-Panzer-Division, after reducing resistance near Poteau, will move into the Vielsalm-Salmchâteau sector. A combat group (including at least one reinforced battalion) will advance in the direction of Grand-Halleux, with the mission of establishing contact with the units of the I. SS-Panzer-Korps fighting in the Stavelot area. After crossing the Salm, the 9. SS-Panzer-Division will advance towards the Ourthe, protecting the northern flank of the advanced units of the 2. SS-Panzer-Division, around Odeigne, while armoured reconnaissance detachments will need to reach Lierneux.*

After being assembled, some of the Tiger units moved towards Bastogne. (*Tegethoff*)

Tiger 312 and at least one other machine faced the 82nd Airborne Division in Goronne. (*NARA*)

The paratroopers were supported by the 740th Tank Battalion. (*NARA*)

The indirect attack by Willi Bittrich's men worked perfectly: most of the 2. SS-Panzer-Division had arrived in the Baraque de Fraiture area when the small American garrison fell, while the 9. SS-Panzer-Division only reached the eastern bank of the Salm. That Christmas night was ideal for the Panzers, with a wonderful moonlight and a hardened snow. The 2. SS-Panzer-Division seized the Manhay crossroads, which was a vital piece of the Americans' new defensive line. However, Heinz Lammerding was not completely satisfied, as only a small part of the opposing armoured column had been neutralized.

For Major General James M. Gavin, commander of the 82nd Airborne Division, withdrawal was inevitable:

> *I had previously been warned by the Corps Commander that we would have to pull out. The orders came at 1330hrs. Tactically, the withdrawal was justified. However, my men raged at having to abandon their positions, realising what it would cost in sweat, suffering and blood when it came to reoccupying each knoll, each spur and each ridge.*

For the Germans, the hour of defeat had come. (*NARA*)

The resistance they envisaged bordered on suicide. I explained this, but I was unable to convince them, and I saw the red anger rise to their foreheads, because they almost believed they were being forced to be deserters. The withdrawal to the Trois-Ponts, Erria, Manhay axis was planned for Christmas night. It was very cold, the moonlight was particularly bright, the snow crunched underfoot, the wind whipped up raging swirls of small crystals that slapped your cheeks.

Covering forces were to remain in place until 0400hrs on 25 December. The withdrawal was facilitated by our 307th Engineer Battalion, who set up hedgehogs, blew up bridges, culverts and footbridges and laid minefields. My 325th and 504th Regiments withdrew without incident. On the other hand, the 508th PIR was attacked in force by the 9. SS-Panzer-Division near the Salm bridges. One of its platoons, installed on the Thier-du-Mont (which runs between Vielsalm and Salmchâteau) was completely surrounded, but managed with great skill and craftsmanship to disengage without losing a single man.

Major Gavin decided to pivot around Trois-Ponts to gain a new frontline. (*NARA*)

Two new M24 light tanks were brought close to the frontlines to show the new equipment to the units in order to avoid mistakes. They were picked up by the 740th Tank Battalion. (*NARA*)

By 2200hrs, the last units of this regiment were assembled at Goronne, except for the rear guard platoons.

At 2300hrs I decided to join the 505th PIR, which was to pivot around Trois-Ponts to reach our new front. At St Jacques I came across a platoon of paratroopers looking for a large German force that had been reported to them. I left for Dairomont, the regimental command post. Indeed, earlier in the evening a driver had noticed heavily armed men heading east in the woods near Basse-Bodeux; some had thrown themselves to the ground, while others scattered for cover. In addition, bullets had hit the jeep of a Signal Corps man who was checking the telephone lines.

Colonel William E. Ekman asked me what he should do: stop the withdrawal and comb the woods to neutralise the German group? Or ignore the enemy presence and continue the withdrawal? The three platoons he had left behind on the Salm as a covering force were beginning to come under heavy pressure from elements of the 1. SS-Panzer-Division, which occupied the other bank. I told him to go ahead with the withdrawal: we had identified at least four divisions that could attack us in the next few hours, so we couldn`t afford to divert a regiment to this new search operation. Our men had to be in place on our new defensive line by daybreak.[3]

The 740th TB fielded M24s in combat for the first time. This one is near Remouchamp. (*NARA*)

Gavin's men had actually encountered the survivors of Peiper's group who were evacuating La Gleize. It was thus the intervention of II. SS-Panzer-Korps and the tactical consequences of its success that saved Peiper from annihilation.

Gavin was not wrong when he said that he would have to recapture all the positions he was forced to abandon, and the recapture of the banks of the Salm began on 3 January 1945. The American attack was tedious: Arbrefontaine did not fall until the evening of the following day. The Shermans of A Company took up position on the high ground south of the village (a promontory that offered a real tactical advantage to the US tanks), from where they were able to block the road from Goronne to Menil. Two days later, 6 January, was quiet according to the report.

It was during this engagement that Tiger 312 was lost. Colonel Rubel, commander of 740th Tank Battalion, attached to Ben Vandervoort's 505th PIR, explains the circumstances of the beast's disablement:

> *My A Company was in support of the 505th PIR, which was to retake Goronne. To protect the left flank, 3rd Platoon moved out from south of Arbrefontaine at 0630hrs. On*

The 740th TB's Shermans were halted by Tiger 312. (*NARA*)

> *the way, it succeeded in neutralizing a dozen machine gun nests, six anti-tank guns, a mortar position, two halftracks loaded with ammunition and various vehicles.*
>
> *Elsewhere, 2nd Platoon launched an attack at 0830hrs. Almost immediately, it came face to face with a Tiger. Disregarding the danger, Sergeant Fasoli fired five shells in quick succession, all of which ricocheted off the turret! Lieutenant Tribby called in two Tank Destroyers for help, but they were turned into torches by the Tiger before they could intervene. Another tank destroyer arrived and, at a distance of just under 150 yards, fired fifteen rounds into the sides of the behemoth before it caught fire. The attack resumed once more. As he entered the village, Sergeant Fasoli encountered a second Panzer VI. He fired two shells, feinted, then fired three more. Again, all bounced off the Panzer's formidable armour, which returned fire three times without hitting the Sherman. A bazooka team* [in reality it was a captured Panzerfaust] *arrived at once, but the monster had 'bravely' withdrawn. The platoon crossed the locality and took up a defensive position on the eastern side.*[4]

The After Action Report of the 740th TB was less triumphant than Rubel's account, instead showing how valiantly the crew of Tiger 312 defended themselves:

M10 Tank Destroyers in action. (*NARA*)

> *2nd Platoon jumped from positions around Arbrefontaine at about 0830hrs. Sergeant Fasoli and Staff Sergeant Hendrix moved forward to attack an enemy Mark VI tank. They manoeuvred and Sergeant Fasoli fired five rounds while Staff Sergeant Hendrix covered. All were direct hits. The turret was jammed, but seeing that they were not going to be able to destroy the Mark VI, Lieutenant Tribby called in two Tank Destroyers (TD). Both were destroyed and set on fire. Lieutenant Tribby then called in another TD and a 57-mm AT gun. Sergeant Fasoli and Lieutenant Tribby drove these guns on foot. The TD fired and set fire to the Mark VI. The infantry fell back and reorganized. Sergeant Fasoli led the attack on the village, followed by Sergeant Hendrix and Lieutenant Tribby. Sergeant Fasoli entered the town under fire. There he encountered a second Mark VI. He fired at it from about 50 yards, hitting it twice, and then retreated to the shelter of a building to fire three more shots. The Mark VI returned fire and missed all three shots. Sergeant Fasoli then destroyed three machine gun nests to the right of his tank. Friendly bazooka teams appeared, but the Mark IV withdrew. The 2nd Platoon crossed the town and took up position on the eastern outskirts.*[5]

The episode shows how difficult was for Shermans to destroy a Tiger tank in single combat in open terrain. The crews could only rely on their experience and manoeuvring

Tiger 312 was finally put out of action. (*NARA*)

Its armour was partly covered with white paint. (*NARA*)

skills, as the American Sherman tanks only had sufficient firepower and manoeuvrability to take on the smaller German tanks. Veteran Cecil Taylor of the 740th TB declared the Shermans were completely outgunned by the Germans' huge Tiger tanks, which were heavily armoured monsters armed with the formidable 88-mm guns.

For Taylor, there was only one way to tackle a Tiger: '*Firstly, you hoped to see it first,*' he said. '*If you came around the corner and ran into one of these things, you were in trouble. We had to attack the Tigers in groups. One tank would hit the tracks to make it stationary, then others would pick it off and tear it apart. We were more manoeuvrable, so once we moved off, they couldn't follow us, but we couldn't go head-to-head with them.*'[6] The only solution for the GIs and tank crews was to join forces. In open country, with exposed terrain such as the pastures between Goronne and Arbrefontaine, calling in the tank destroyers was the best option. Rubel's account is dismissive and intended to highlight the action of his battalion, so it must be seen for what it is: a directed source. The second Tiger in the village had no chance without its infantry cover. Paratroopers of the 505th PIR, equipped with a stolen Panzerfaust, would have had the clear advantage.

Note that it was also during the attack on Goronne that Lieutenant Colonel Benjamin H. Vandervoort, the commander of II/505th PIR (played by John Wayne in the film 'The Longest Day'), was seriously wounded by a mortar shell explosion, which ended his military career.

Rubel's account mentions two Tigers: the first was set on fire, while the second retreated. There is no trace of fire in the photograph of Tiger 312, so this must have been the one that was forced to retreat.

Used in small groups, the Tiger was engaged outside its normal deployment methods. (*NARA*)

This episode also involves the fact that on 7 January, 1. SS-Panzer-Abteilung 501 was still in the northern sector. On 8 January, the unit still had thirty operational vehicles and was engaged in occasional actions for units of Heeresgruppe B. An interesting detail is that in the wreckage of one of the tanks destroyed during the battle, a US intelligence report states that it belonged to the battalion's Stab. The information was disseminated in the Periodic Report of the G2 of the 1st Infantry Division, 30 kilometres away, and the map coordinates of Goronne were given, thus allowing us to identify Tiger 312 without error.[7] However, the information was corrected a little later when the Americans finally understood that they were facing a corps unit.

Tiger 331: Isolated in Bizory

As mentioned in Chapter 1, an armoured Kampfgruppe supported the lines of the 340. Volksgrenadier-Division to intervene in case of a US breakthrough. Two Tigers of s. SS-Pz-Abt 501 were included in this group.

Reinforcements arrive in the Bastogne area. (*NARA*)

An offensive towards Houffalize is prepared. (*NARA*)

The German troops in the Bastogne sector had already suffered heavy losses. (NARA)

The initial assault of 340. VGD began on 3 January 1945. It was successful and shook the 6th Armored Division for a while, but its lines resisted well and the German attacker was finally pushed back to the high ground around Bizory.

A destroyed Tiger tank with numbering relating to s. SS-Pz-Abt 501 was photographed in this area, although the caption simply says, 'Bizory'. Knowing that two tanks were operating in this area, the After Action Reports of units known to have fought there in the first half of January were consulted. When the 6th AD went back on the attack, it was supported in this sector by infantrymen of the III/320th Infantry Regiment, 35th ID. The battalion's After Action Report mentions on 9 January: '*Artillery and mortar fire fell in the advanced sector. At 1310 hours five tanks were reported in the vicinity of point 586606. One of these was disabled by artillery fire. Patrols at the front are in contact with the enemy.*'[8]

The coordinates correspond to a point 2 kilometres north-east of Bizory, specifically in the area where 340. VGD was operating at that time. From these coordinates it was relatively easy to find the location where Tiger 331 was photographed, which was 300 metres to the east, not far from the small wood of Arloncourt. We were lucky enough to

Patton's aim was to turn Bastogne into a springboard to close the salient. (*NARA*)

At the beginning of January, the Americans went on the offensive. (*NARA*)

The first photograph identified in the Bizory sector was the beginning of our investigation. (*Rights reserved*)

have photographs taken in two opposite directions, which allowed us to find the location of the Tiger's destruction.

From a tactical point of view, while the Tiger-Abteilungen had great capabilities in terms of passive defence, such as at Goronne, it was during counter-attacks that they could show their worth. German regulations stated that, where possible, counter-attacks should be carefully planned and were to be launched as soon as the opportunity arose. Nevertheless, the depth of the attack was limited, and it was only used to re-establish the continuity of a defensive line and did not go beyond that. When it came to stopping an assault, the rules of engagement were different.

The Panzerwaffe had a special term for this kind of manoeuvre: the *Gegenstoss*, which could be translated as 'counter-assault'. In this case, it was a reactive mission launched in an emergency, the aim being to restore a critical situation or to repel an enemy assault. There was therefore no planning, let alone any elaborate reconnaissance, for the engagement, and it was generally done within the means available to the commander in place by agglomerating the available units. The advantage of such a tactic meant you benefitted from the element of surprise. An Allied unit that advanced into battle and sensed the enemy's line was about to break had no idea that it would soon face a powerful, heavy tank counter-attack.

A photograph of the same machine allowed us to discover that it was a tank of the s. SS-Pz-Abt 501, commanded by Rolf von Westernagen. (*Rights reserved*)

The SS-Pz-Abt 501 had already demonstrated in Normandy how effective it could be in such a situation, and from the American report, it seems that Tiger 331 was engaged in just such a manoeuvre. An interesting detail is that the machine was commanded by Rolf von Westernhagen, who was none other than the younger brother of Heinz von Westernhagen, the commander of the Abteilung.

Photographic analysis reveals several things: it is the only tank destroyed in the area; artillery fire burnt its left flank; and the heat had deformed the torsion bars of the suspension. The result was clear to see: the chassis had sunk onto its running gear. A later shot also shows the vehicle's number, but also the fact that it was later targeted by an anti-tank gun.

Rolf von Westernagen was the younger brother of Heinz von Westernhagen, the commander of the Abteilung. (*Rights reserved*)

The Unknown of Lutrebois

Another photograph has come down to us from a book published in 1974.[9] The caption states that the machine was photographed at Lutrebois, after the recapture of the village. The area where the tank was destroyed, on the heights east of Lutrebois, along the edge

Taken from a different angle, this photograph enabled us to identify the precise location of the wreck. (*Rights reserved*)

The high ground around the village of Lutrebois was hotly contested by the SS and the 35th Infantry Division. (*NARA*)

The only known photograph of the Lutrebois Tiger was published in a 1974 book. (*Louis Lefebvre*)

of a pine wood overlooking the village, was cleared on 12 January 1945 by the II/134th IR of the 35th ID.[10] Curiously, there is no mention of the machine in the reports of the unit or the regiment to which it belonged. The report by 654th TD, which was engaged in the sector in support of the infantry battalion, also fails to mention the presence of a Tiger.

The absence of apparent markings on the machine means we are unable to provide more detail on this illustrious stranger, except that it is not in the sector where the s. SS-Panzer-Abteilung 506 saw action, around Bastogne. As the history of the 1. SS-Panzer-Division does not mention the presence of a Tiger in its counter-attack, it was therefore probably supporting the 167. Volksgrenadier-Division, and was likely put out of action between 8 and 12 January 1945.

As research continues on this unknown monster from Lutrebois, let us hope that in a future edition of this book, additional elements will allow us to say more.

A Very Special Battalion

Tiger 304 is an unknown whose existence was revealed to us by an American historian who unearthed photographs of a Tiger in the Ardennes taken by men of B Battery, 987th Field Artillery Battalion (FAB). This was a field artillery battalion with 155-mm self-propelled guns mounted on Sherman chassis, in fact, an M12 Gun Motor Carriage according to the American terminology. This battalion left Camp Bowie, Texas, on 17 February 1944 to begin its journey to Europe in preparation for the Normandy landings. It arrived without its equipment at Greenock, Scotland, on 22 March and received its self-propelled guns in England on 2 May, just in time to prepare them for action at the time of the D-Day landings.

The battalion was a corps-independent unit attached to units on the battlefield according to the needs of the time. Thus, it began its campaign on European soil in support of the British 50th Infantry Division within the 5th Army Group Royal Artillery of the 2nd British Army, who were involved in the operations to capture Caen. On 30 June 1944, the 987th FAB returned to American command and was attached to V Corps, with whom it worked for most of the liberation campaign. In autumn 1944 the battalion was in the Hurtgen Forest sector, supporting American units as they struggled to cross the Siegfried Line. It must be said that this artillery battalion was furnished with equipment that was unusual in the American army, with most of the 155-mm 'long tom' tubes being deployed in towed form. The GMC M12 was a self-propelled artillery gun, with similar mobility to a tank, allowing it to operate in a different way to conventional long tom guns. It was able to approach concrete pillboxes and fire at them almost at point blank range. The heavy howitzer was, one suspects, very effective in this bunker buster role. Consequently, it would remain in the northern region of the Ardennes to support V Corps in its offensive on Moschau, beginning on 13 December 1944.[11]

When the Ardennes offensive started, V Corps sent reinforcements to fight the northern flank of the German breakthrough, which is why these artillerymen were in the area where s. SS-Panzer-Abteilung 501 was operating. The 987th FAB was attached to the 30th ID between 26 December 1944 and 14 January 1945 to support it in its fight to recapture the Malmedy plateau.[12] For the first time in the Western European campaign, its batteries were brought together to operate as a unit. During this terrible battle, the artillerymen occupied two firing positions: Ster and Ondeval. On the assumption that the gunners photographed the machine close to their firing positions, it is logical to assume the machine was located in one of these two locations.

Ster's scenario is eliminated from the outset for the simple reason that the Tigers could not have passed through there on their way to Stavelot due to the routes they would have needed to take. Ondenval, on the other hand, was on the route taken by the heavy tanks at the start of the offensive. It is possible, however, that at the end of the Battle of Bastogne, at the time of the withdrawal to St Vith, the surviving tanks also withdrew via this village. It is therefore much more likely, in our view, that the machine was photographed in this area.

The US advance was unstoppable. (*NARA*)

The fighting was concentrated in the St Vith sector. (*NARA*)

The 987th Field Artillery Battalion was equipped with Gun Motor Carriage M12, a Sherman chassis with a 155-mm gun. (*NARA*)

An analysis of the available photographs reveals many details: The number 304 is clearly visible; the left track is missing, and the Schurzen dismantled; wooden debris is placed on the left side; and the machine gun seems to be missing. Such details provide clues as to what happened to the vehicle. The tank's immobilisation was clearly due to a broken track, and the crew obviously tried to repair it by first removing the undercarriage protections. The immobilised vehicle was partly camouflaged by a few planks, probably with the aim of breaking the silhouette in a defensive tactical configuration. Meanwhile, the absence of the main machine gun indicates a forced abandonment by its occupants.

The surrounding terrain reveals that the tank is on flat ground, with slight relief in the background, and an elongated building with a chimney on the right-hand side of the roof is visible. A post can be seen to the rear at the level of the half barrel, and the left-hand side is bordered by a tall hedge. After having made a sketch of the site, analysis of the IGN maps from 1925 and 1956 indicates a possible location for the tank. Arriving at the scene, these details were soon identified and by comparing the IGN maps and the photographs, we quickly confirmed the location: the hedges, its plantation, the sloping ground, the house with the chimney, an electric post, everything matched perfectly. This result shows once again that serious preliminary research in the archives means later disappointments can be avoided.

The unit usually fought in separate batteries. (*NARA*)

It is true that the SS-Pz-Abt 501 twice passed through the sector. However, on 26 December, in preparation for the counter-attack in the Bastogne sector, all salvageable damaged vehicles were collected. If the vehicle had been lost before that date, it is likely that it would have been recovered, given the damage to the track, which was in theory easily repairable. It is therefore more likely that the vehicle was lost later, between 10 and 15 January.

With the location identified and the date presumed, further archive research was carried out. An aerial photographic analysis report of 14 January 1945, requested by

It was during the Battle of the Bulge that the 987th Field Artillery Battalion fought for the first time. (*NARA*)

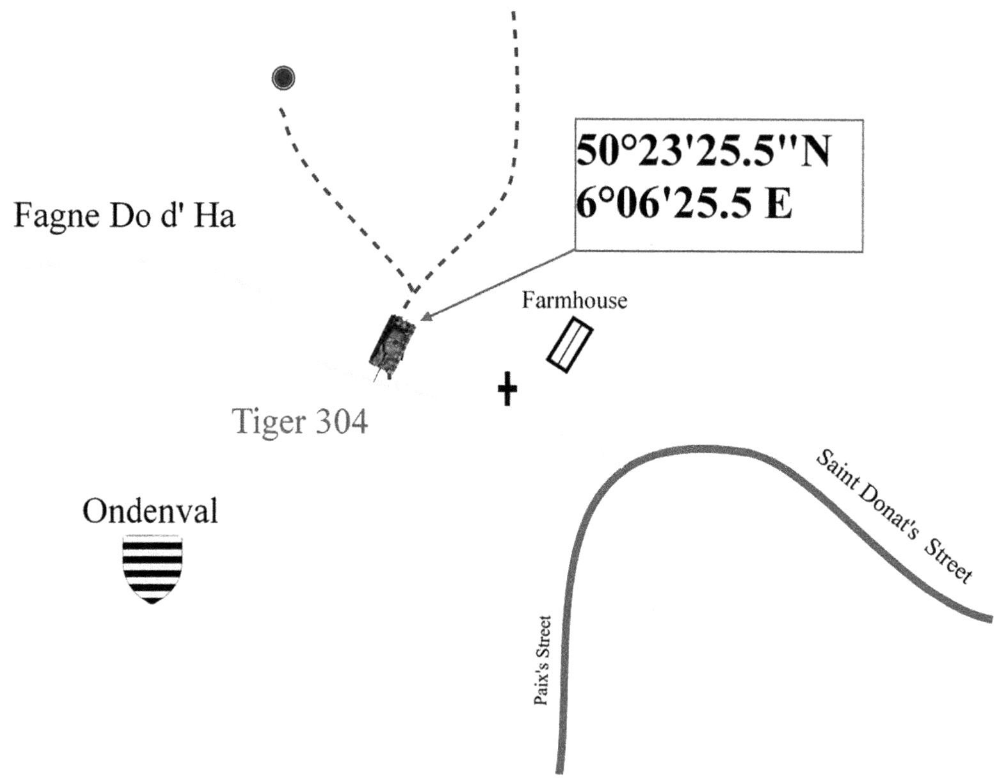

Map showing the position of Tiger 304. (*Authors' collection*)

The 30th ID attacked in the Thirimont sector. (*NARA*)

XVIII Airborne Corps, indicated a possible tank at this location, giving the coordinates 8446/0065.[13] A gully close by (in reality the bed of the stream that runs right through this spot) provided the perfect position to prohibit any armoured breakthrough into the valley south of Ondenval. This archival confirmation fully validated our research hypothesis, but to understand the fate of the machine, we need to immerse ourselves in the battle for this sector.

The German Retreat

On 10 January 1945, the elements in the frontline at Bastogne belonging to s. SS-Pz-Abt 501 received the order to withdraw from Lutremange-Villers la Bonne Eau and head towards St Vith.[14] The town was a crucial crossroads, so its defence was vitally important to allow the withdrawal of the 6. Panzer-Armee.[15] Ondenval now became a crucial point of resistance. On the same date, a report from 5th AD HQ indicated an upsurge of activity in the sector, but only small groups were reported.[16] For the time being, Fallschirmjäger from the 3.FJD were identified in the vicinity, with III/Fallschirmjäger-Regiment (FJR) 9 having set up its command post in the village.[17] Some of the elements under its command, however, had belonged to 8 FJR since 2 January.[18] The German paratroopers were ordered to hold their position at all costs, despite the difficult logistical situation whereby the division received its supplies by sledge.[19] A little to the south, the

The Fallschirmjäger of III/Fallschirmjäger-Regiment (FJR), 3.FJD, were identified in this area. (NAC)

The snow made tactical manoeuvres difficult. (*NAC*)

G2 of the 30th ID reported that in the Ligneuville sector, a main line of resistance was being formed in the form of a series of small resistance points on the opposite slopes of the valleys, with firing ranges facilitating the use of automatic weapons.[20] Meanwhile, elements of the 18. VGD were reported at Baugnez.

Ondenval was on the border of two American corps. To the north was V Corps, with the 1st Infantry Division, and to the east was XVIII Airborne Corps, the umbrella of the 30th ID which was advancing from Stavelot. Thus, the village was threatened to the north by the advance of the 1st ID, with the 16th Infantry Regiment also in the area, while the 30th ID was advancing towards Ligneuville. V Corps artillery spotted several tanks in the village (a Zug of five and two isolated vehicles), which it engaged in the early afternoon of 10 January.[21] The next day, American intelligence reported considerable traffic in the village,[22] which was a preferred withdrawal route for troops evacuating the Ardennes salient. On 11 January, V Corps reported that Ondenval was crossed by a few tanks and self-propelled vehicles, and the Americans believed that the place was being transformed into a resistance centre.[23] This was confirmed the next day by the 30th ID, which identified a line of outposts running from the heights south of Houffalize to Baugnez, with a main line of resistance set up a little to the south, at Ondenval.[24] On 13 January, the 23rd Combat Team (CT) of the 2nd Infantry Division 'Indian' was attached to the 1st ID, charged with operating on the right wing of the division and taking particular care of the right flank, which was fighting a few kilometres to the north.

The area was stormed from 14 January. West of the village, Thirimont was fiercely defended and gave the 120th IR of the 30th ID a hard time. The next day, after having

The artillery of the 2nd Infantry Division went into action in the area. (*NARA*)

been ejected from the village during the night of the 14th, the GIs regained their foothold. The 16th IR of the 1st ID was still held up in front of Faymonville, while the 23rd CT still had to capture the heights south of Waimes.

On the evening of 15 January, Ondenval had not yet fallen into American hands. The frontline reported by 30th ID passed precisely through the coordinates of Tiger 304, which appeared to be reinforcing the position there. The 30th ID G2 report describes the German defensive method:

> *The enemy is defending the heights south of the Amblève, using a large quantity of anti-tank mines on both main and secondary roads. Resistance points, held by infantry, are camouflaged in wooded areas with fields of fire directed at the approach roads and firebreaks in the forest areas. In the town itself, it uses the buildings to house automatic weapons.*

II/23rd CT/ 30th ID went on the attack from the northern sector of Ondenval. (*NARA*)

The report further states that the defenders of the village were reinforced by six tank hunters belonging to 348. Panzerjäger-Abteilung,[25] an independent unit.

On 16 January, the II/23rd TC went on the attack from the north. During the night, it heard vehicles temporarily start their engines, a habit of German tankers to recharge the batteries. The US battalion was in the immediate vicinity of Tiger 304's position, and so it is conceivable that this is our vehicle. At 0800hrs, the leading elements of the II/23rd CT approached the northern edge of Ondenval. The village was attacked by a clamp, with F Coy attacking from the north-east, E Coy in the centre and G Coy from the west. At 0813hrs they entered the main crossroads, about 400 metres south-west of Tiger 304. From the operation reports it seems that the town had been abandoned the night

US infantry pursued the enemy and passed Tiger 304 without seeing it. (*NARA*)

before.[26] At 1035hrs, however, G Coy reported that as it entered the town, two Panzers fired at them from the high ground. Two M10s from the 612th TD were in support on the heights of Remonval on the hillside opposite the village. The tank hunters took aim at the two German machines in their sights, and the crews believed they had hit one of the tanks present. At 1125hrs, German resistance ceased in Ondenval.[27] The 23rd TC did not linger in the village and the pursuit of the enemy continued in the direction of St Vith, along the main road. Tiger 304 was, in fact, stopped at the junction of the 23rd CT and the 120th IR of the 30th ID. Hidden behind a hedge on a secondary road, it went completely unnoticed by the two large units and was later discovered by the gunners of the 987th FAB.

The operational accounts do not mention the Panzer as such. However, we can assume that it arrived in the area around 12 or 13 January and that on the 14th, it was in position on the heights of Ondenval, acting as an anchor point for the German lines. Although it was admirably positioned, it did not have a target in its field of fire until the morning of the 16th. It was most likely already immobilised when Ondenval was evacuated the night

It was the coordination of infantry with tanks that allowed the Americans to emerge victorious. (*NARA*)

before and it is possible that the crew stayed behind to try to save their precious Tiger, which had suffered only minor damage, although it was virtually impossible to repair without the pulling power of a maintenance vehicle. It may have been the 304's engine that was heard during the night before the assault and that its machine guns spoke one last time on the morning of 16 January. In the absence of more precise German sources, it is impossible for us to know more.

Conclusion: Autopsy of a Fiasco

Insufficient preparation

The secret of the *Wacht am Rhein* operation was so closely guarded that the plans finalised in October 1944 were not communicated to the generals responsible for carrying it out until five days before the action was to take place. Everything had to be planned down to the last detail, but staff work at the tactical level was clearly insufficient. Peiper was ordered to charge forward without regard to his flanks, while the reconnaissance unit that followed him was given the task of securing the route. Unfortunately, there was too much time between the passage of the Spitze[1] and its continuation, and the Americans reacted with a magnificent swiftness that isolated the head of the unit. There was, it seems, poor coordination between the different Kampfgruppen of the 'Leibstandarte', which a more thorough preparation at regimental level could have potentially resolved.

KG Peiper lost almost all its tanks, with the Panther and Panzer IV suffering even more losses than the Tiger. (*NARA*)

American artillery strongly hindered the German operations. (*NARA*)

When Peiper was interviewed after the war, he was asked what he would have done differently, and his answer essentially focused on this aspect of the problem:

> *It soon became clear that the real aim of the Ardennes counter-offensive was not to reach Antwerp, but simply to disrupt the American preparations and delay the winter offensive by two months. This should have been made clear by the High Command before the fighting began. There are some things I would have liked to have done differently:*
>
> *a) Instituted a faster refuelling system.*
> *b) Had no artillery preparation and kept the horse batteries out of the way.*
> *c) Attacked with combat teams and tanks at the same time as infantry (an unsupported infantry attack wastes too much time).*
> *d) Reduced the length of each column: instead of two or three Kampfgruppen, cut the formation into twenty small segments. In this way, regrouping would have been easier in the face of any enemy action.*
> *e) Used more infantry on tanks.*
> *f) Carried pontoon boat units with each armoured formation.*
> *g) Made each combat team self-sufficient.*
> *h) Put a general on every street corner to regulate traffic.*[2]

German fighters did not have time to prepare for their missions. (*Rights reserved*)

Lack of fuel

Indeed, fuel was the main cause of Peiper's failure. If he blamed himself for not having planned a sufficient logistical flow to supply his vehicles, it is clear that the problem already existed at higher levels. Fuel was a general problem before the offensive, and the units were insufficiently supplied with appropriate stock before the attack.

On this subject, in the report of an inspection tour on 31 December 1944, Albert Speer wrote to Hitler:

> *Transport… can only be carried out with all lights off. The difficulties of night transport and the impossibility of daytime traffic mean that, with an equivalent road network, our traffic is half or two-thirds less than that of the enemy, who can drive by day almost without being bothered and drive at night with their lights on. Moreover, the state of the roads in the Eifel and Ardennes constitutes another very serious difficulty, especially for the transport of reinforcements… Most of the roads have hills and bends, meaning traffic difficulties there are as great as on a mountain road… The strategy devised by the Supreme Command and the orders derived from it are certainly not always adapted to the*

The lack of fuel was fatal for KG Peiper. (*NARA*)

> *supply problems resulting from this situation. Supply seems to be of secondary importance in the preparation of operations... When supply is not taken into account and calculated properly, the operation is bound to fail.*[3]

Peiper's unit had only two petrol tanks before going into battle in an area where consumption would be five times higher than normal. One or two extra measures carried in jerrycans would have avoided the risk of having a diminishing margin of manoeuvre as the battle wore on.

Due to lack of fuel and after an unsuccessful attempt to refuel by air, the Kampfgruppe was finally forced to abandon all its equipment in the Kessel (cauldron) and sneak back to the German lines on foot. Deprived of its initial refuelling and its supply route cut off, the gargantuan appetite of its beasts was largely responsible for this costly decision in terms of equipment. A Panther consumed between 350 and 700 litres of fuel per 100 kilometres, while the Tiger II needed between 750 and 1,100 litres. Tiger Nos. 104, 204, 211, 221 and 332, almost 50 percent of the total strength of the troops beyond the Amblève, were lost due to lack of fuel.

Allied tactical aviation played havoc with the communication lines. (*NARA*)

A Task Against the Doctrine

It is an obvious fact when analysing the organisation of the armoured column that the use of the Tiger was planned in a way that was heretical to the doctrine of how it should be deployed.

Firstly, the s. SS-Panzer-Abteilung 501 was a heavy armoured battalion. These formations used specific equipment and were therefore very different from the medium armour used by the Panzer-Division. Such specialised formations were supposed to work independently for one-off actions on the front when the need arose. In theory, a Panzer-Division had a Panzer-Regiment with two medium tank Abteilungen. The losses of autumn 1944 did not allow the 1. SS-Pz-Div to regain the levels of these theoretical numbers. This meant the Tigers were therefore there to make up the shortfall and not to be used according to their specific characteristics. Admittedly, Peiper envisaged putting them at the forefront after the crossing of the Meuse, where their thick armour and 88-mm KwK 43 L/71 gun would have given them a considerable advantage in open terrain, meaning they could push back any American machines they came into contact

German Flak was not powerful enough to counter-attack. (*Jacobs Bibliothèque de Stavelot*)

with. Although this idea was not bad in itself, it was based on a misunderstanding of the conditions of how the schwere Panzer-Abteilungen should be used.

Due to their equipment, these highly specialised formations required specific methods of use. The delicate mechanics of the machines and their logistical requirements placed them in a similar tactical configuration to the British rhombohedral tanks of the First World War. After a maximum of 24 hours of action, they needed to be withdrawn from the frontline for extensive maintenance before returning to combat. Given the speed of the breakthrough, such thorough maintenance was impossible. Worse still, the heavy equipment was placed in the lead Kampfgruppe, a position inaccessible to the maintenance echelons traditionally placed in the division's rear column. Equipment which the crews were unable to repair themselves was irretrievably lost if they were forced to abandon any conquered terrain.

The Tiger was designed to be a breakthrough tank, another similarity it shared with the British Mark IVs of 1917, whose mission was to break through the enemy's frontline. They were intended to operate in the Hesbaye region, more than 100 kilometres from their home base. This was mechanically impossible and was a well-known issue, being the cause of the misadventure of the s. Pz-Abt 508, which was in charge of the Allied bridgehead at Anzio. Due to logistical complications and American air superiority, the machines were unloaded from the train 200 kilometres from their engagement zone. As in the Ardennes a year later, the road was difficult to negotiate. The gradients were enormous, causing the engines to overheat, while the many bends put a strain on the tanks' highly sensitive transmissions. Sixty percent of them broke down during the transfer to the front. The Abteilung arrived on the battlefield in small packs and although the majority of them eventually made it to the front, the engines suffered enormously and the breakdown rate was consequently very high. The largest strike force the battalion could muster at any one time was thirty tanks. The problem was compounded by the fact that some of the Panzer VIs broke down in an area where recovery was difficult, as the

Having run out of fuel, the SS evacuated La Gleize on foot. (*NARA*)

region was under fire from Allied warships – a problem not dissimilar to the one that the 501 would later encounter when it came under constant enemy artillery shelling.

A Tiger weighed 69 tonnes, while a Panther was almost 25 tonnes lighter, meaning the route restrictions imposed even in terms of deck class were much more severe. In theory, the routes chosen needed to allow the Tiger to move in the best possible conditions, but such precautions are obviously impossible to meet during a deep breakthrough, and during an operation where speed of action was paramount. To make matters worse, the routes chosen were via very bad roads. While it is true that these machines were very impressive, their 69 tonnes and long 88-mm KwK 43 L/71 gun made them very difficult to manoeuvre on the narrow Ardennes roads, where their gargantuan fuel consumption would prove to be a very significant logistical burden.

Finally, it is difficult to understand why the Tiger battalions were not put in the frontline during the initial assault on 16 December. Breaking through the American front would have been a task worthy of them, and such a punch given at the start of the offensive would probably have enabled a more rapid collapse of the US frontlines. Leaving the exploitation to the medium tanks would have allowed the selection of the best possible routes for the heavies and avoided this loss of cohesion.

The Tigers required constant maintenance. (*NAC*)

A Revealing Balance Sheet

When adding up the causes of failure, a sample of eighteen vehicles found on the battlefield after the event can be identified:

- Five were lost in action.
- Six were immobilised because they ran out of fuel.
- Five were lost directly or indirectly due to mechanical problems.[4]
- One was lost as a result of an air attack.
- One was lost due to unknown causes (Lutrebois).

On 15 January, when the Abteilung assembled in Blankenheim, it had only ten operational machines left.[5] The others were either being repaired or had been lost without trace. Assuming that only the eighteen machines were really lost, twenty-seven would thus be available for combat. This was far from the truth, with seventeen Tigers lost for reasons unknown to us. If we extrapolate the number of unavailable Tigers to the known losses for mechanical or logistical reasons, it is reasonable to think that 72 percent of the seventeen missing tigers, i.e. between twelve and thirteen, were lost through attrition that had nothing to do with any genuine combat. The fiasco is now even more obvious.

In the end, only 28 percent of Tiger losses were due to direct enemy action; the rest were caused by the unsuitability of the vehicles for the areas they were deployed in. Too fragile and too greedy, they were more of a burden than a real help to Peiper. Paradoxically, the officers of the 'Leibstandarte' operated their machines well. Peiper placed them at the back of the column with the aim of getting them into the fight when their range would be useful beyond the Meuse. Yet the fog of war, amplified by insufficient preparation, resulted in them being at the front. Peiper made good use of the superior range of the 88-mm gun to blockade the valley, while Tiger 334 was used as a breakthrough machine. Meanwhile, Knittel made excellent use of the three Tigers at his disposal: Tiger 332 at Goronne gave the 740th TB a hard time, while 331 and 131 were victims of US artillery.

It is one thing to build a virtually invulnerable machine, but quite another to make it an effective combat vehicle on any battlefield. The Tiger, particularly the second model, paid the price for its sophistication and weight. Too heavy, too wide and too greedy, it was ineffective on the Ardennes battlefield, where the roads were narrow and winding. The steep inclines out of the valleys placed a lot of strain on the sprockets of its undersized gearbox, and as soon as it had to move, the vehicle was handicapped. Its firepower was useless in the Ardennes, where the compartmentalisation of the terrain meant range was only 500 metres on average, and even then only when the weather was good. In this case, having a gun capable of firing at 2 kilometres was completely useless. Worse still, the Tiger's fuel consumption created insurmountable difficulties for the logistical services, which were obliged to obtain supplies from beyond the Rhine, and who were continually harassed by the Allied tactical aviation. The Tiger II had too little opportunity to demonstrate its advantages in the Ardennes. The losses of the schwere

SS-Panzer- Abteilung 501 in the Stavelot sector, where the vast majority of its machines were lost to mechanical or supply issues, are a glaring example. The adventures of the Tigers from KG Peiper demonstrate in abundance the incompatibility of the weapon system with the mission it was assigned. The long and winding routes imposed on the machines generated a mechanical attrition that was as enormous as it was inevitable. This resulted in disorder in the heavy battalion's column, which immediately lost its cohesion. Too greedy to be supplied in sufficient quantities, its tanks were reduced to serving as immobile bunkers at a time when they could have been used, for example, to obtain a breakthrough at Targnon. In fact, lining up the Tiger II in the Ardennes ultimately had serious consequences for the German army by needlessly increasing an already unmanageable logistical burden. The Third Reich would have done better to send them eastwards to more favourable sectors, where their unique attributes could have been much more effective.

A Tiger acting on its own had little chance of achieving results. (*NARA*)

Notes

Chapter 1

1. Washington, NARA, ETHINT 10, p. 8.
2. Bouwmester H., *Beginning of the End: the Leadership of SS-Obersturmbannführer Jochen Peiper*, Fort Leavenworth, Kansas 2004, p. 72.
3. Washington, NARA, Atrocity Trial Testimony Lt Col Peiper. Chapter IV, p. 2.
4. Cuppens, G., *Massacre à Malmedy? Ardennes: 17 Decembre 1944*, Bayeux, 1989, p. 38.
5. Washington, NARA, ETHINT 10, p. 2.
6. Laby, H., *Ardennes 44 Stavelot*, Faimes, 1999, pp. 52-7.
7. Washington, NARA, ETHINT 10, p. 18.
8. See DUJARDIN C.h., *La Bataille des Dépôts*, in MOOK 1944, No.7, 2021, pp. 98-114.
9. Washington, NARA, Atrocity Trial Testimony Lt Col Peiper. Chapter IV, p. 5.
10. Washington, NARA, no date of entry, S3 journal history, 743rd Tank Battalion 1 Nov- 31 Dec, pp. 127-8.
11. For more details, see DUJARDIN C.h., *La Bataille des Dépôts*, in MOOK 1944, n° 7, 2021, pp. 98-114
12. Speer, L., *110th AAA Driving Hitler's Crawlin' Coffin*, Bloomington, 2006, pp. 194-5.
13. The A-2 is the second tank destroyer of Company A.
14. Washington, NARA, AAR 1 31 December, 823rd Tank Destroyer Battalion.
15. Sherman number 10 of C Company, 743rd TB.
16. Paratroopers.
17. Staff Sergeant in the SS.
18. Washington, NARA, AAR 1 31 December, 823rd Tank Destroyer Battalion.
19. In reality, holding Cheneux was imperative for the Germans.
20. According to veterans of the 504th PIR interviewed by Mr Christian Dujardin, it seems that the TDs remained at a "respectable distance" from the engagement, which did not prevent them from giving appreciable support by distant fire.
21. These were actually the traditional fence wires that closed off the pastures.
22. Gavin, J., *On to Berlin*, New York, 1978, pp. 223-4.
23. The Boutet house.
24. This battalion and the character of Cook were immortalised in the film 'A Bridge Too Far' when the unit rowed across the Rhine in daylight under fire from the Germans. Robert Redford played the role of Cook.
25. Cuppens G., op. cit. pp. 63-4.
26. Washington, NARA, Atrocity Trial Testimony Lt Col Peiper. Chapter IV, p. 9.
27. Grégoire, G., *Les Panzer de Peiper face à l'US Army*, Stavelot, 1986, pp. 25-6.
28. The G4 dealt with logistical issues within a divisional headquarters.
29. Probably G4 at the top level.
30. Fort Leavenworth, Ike Skelton Library, 30th ID G4 report, entry of 24/12/1944.
31. Fort Leavenworth, Ike Skelton Library, 30th ID Artillery report, entry of 24/12/1944.
32. Washington, NARA, T78 roll 314, Tagesmeldung OB West, entry of 27/12/1944.
33. Diekirch, National Museum of Military History, testimony of Diether Kuhlman (6. Komp/II/SS Pz-Rgt 1), p. 6.

34. Freiburg, Bundes Archives, MSA 926, p. 5.
35. Testimony of Tielman, interviewed by Frank Rockenbrod.
36. Schneider, W., *Tigers in Combat, vol. II*, Mechanicsburg, 1998, p. 216.
37. Kleine, E. and Kühn, V., *Tiger: the History of a Legendary Weapon 1942-45*, Manitoba, 1989, p. 219.
38. Washington, NARA, MSA 877, Hermann Preiss report on the use of I. SS-Panzer-Korps during the Battle of the Bulge, pp.57-8.
39. Tiemann,R., *The Leibstandarte, Vol. IV/2*, Winnipeg, 1998, pp. 155-7.
40. Washington, NARA, op. cit., p. 59.
41. Ibid, pp. 60-2.

Chapter 2

1. Jentz, T., *The Complete Guide to the Creation & Combat Employment of German's Tank Force, 1933-1942*, Atglen, Pennsylvania, 1996. p. 220.
2. Gudgin, P., *The Tiger Tanks*, London, 1991, p. 91.
3. Schneider, W., op. cit., p. 204.
4. Washington, Library of Congress, GUIDES TO GERMAN RECORDS MICROFILMED AT ALEXANDRIA, VA No. 75. Records of the Waffen-SS, Part I, pp. 8-11.
5. Washington, NARA, RG 242 T78 R719, Part 1. Meldung 1/1/1944 SS schwere Panzer Abteilung 101.
6. Rank equivalent to captain.
7. Rank equivalent to 1st lieutenant.
8. Recovery tank on a Panzer V Panther chassis.
9. Washington, NARA, Rg 242 T78 op. cit., p. 65.
10. Located 2 kilometres north-east of Villers-Bocage.
11. Agte, P., *Michael Wittmann and the Waffen SS Tigers Commanders of the Leibstandarte in WW II, Vol II*, Mecanicsburg, 2006, p. 15.
12. Schneider W., op.cit., p. 214.
13. Ibid, p. 257.
14. Wilbeck W., *Sledgehammers, Strengths and Flaws of Tiger Battalions in World War II*, Bedford Pennsylvania,2004, p. 186.

Chapter 3

1. Interview with Werner Wendt by George Wendt in 1991, quoted in the *Official Bulletin of the International Research Center for the Battle of the Bulge* (criba), No. 3, 2003, pp. 6-9.
2. Ibid.
3. Ibid.
4. Wilson, A., *Leap Off, 404th Fighter Group Combat History*, no place, no date, p. 124.
5. Washington, NARA, AAR 825th TD bat, entry of 18/12/1944.
6. Probably Tiger 104, the only armoured vehicle of 1. Kompagnie to have been found at La Gleize.
7. Wijers H., *Die Ardennen-Offensive: Die Brücken von Stavelot und Trois-Ponts, Das Schicksal des Kampfgruppe Peiper*, no place, no date , p. 160.
8. AP: Armor piercing shell.
9. This may seem like a surprising number, but it is actually the conversion of a 1,000-yard distance.
10. 'Back! Back!'
11. The road surface was made of local cobblestones, which became slippery in a fine drizzle. On these wet stones, the steel of the caterpillar tracks offered little grip.
12. *The Tiger Combat Manual*, D656/27, Die Tiger fibel,s.l., s.d., pp. 20-30.
13. Laby, H., op. cit. p. 342.
14. Probably the famous Hotel des Ardennes.
15. Interview with Werner Wendt by George Wendt, op. cit., pp. 6-9.
16. The grooves are still visible on the facades at the top of the street today.

17. Interview with Werner Wendt by George Wendt, op. cit., pp. 6-9.
18. 'Verify' was the nickname of the 743rd Tank Battalion.
19. Robinwon, W. and Hamilton, N., *Move Out, Verify: the Combat Story of the 743rd Tank Battalion*, United States Army, pp. 124-5.
20. Cofer l., *The Bridge at Stavelot*, website www.Criba.be, accessed on 15 March 2014.
21. Laby, H., op. cit. p. 235.
22. Interview with Werner Wendt by George Wendt, op cit., pp. 6-9.
23. Ibid.
24. American tankers were well trained to recognize the different types of German tanks, referring to the Panzerkampfwagen VI Tiger II as Mark VI.
25. Fort Leavenworth, Ike Skelton Library, S3 Journal 743rd Tank Battalion, entry of 20/12/1944.
26. Interview by Christian Dujardin with Mr Jacques Crahay, May 2014.
27. Interview with Werner Wendt by George Wendt, op. cit., pp. 6-9.
28. Cofer l., *The Bridge at Stavelot*, website www.Criba.be, accessed on 15 March 2014.

Chapter 4

1. Testimony collected by Christian Dujardin from Mr Gérard Grégoire in May 2014, who stated that the building destroyed in the fire was not rebuilt.
2. Ibid.
3. Washington, NARA, Atrocity Trial Testimony Lt Col Peiper. Chapter IV, pp. 7–8.
4. Mill stop group.
5. Cuppens, G., op. cit., p. 74.
6. Fontaine, S., *Stoumont Cheneux La Gleize December 1944*, no place, no date, p. 43.
7. Washington, NARA, no date of entry, 117th unit journal December 1944, p. 46.
8. Testimony of First Lieutenant Joseph A. Couri, quoted in the *Official Bulletin of the International Research Center for the Battle of the Bulge*, No. 3, 1992, pp. 16-20.
9. Fort Leavenworth, Ike Skelton Library, After Action Report 743rd TB, entry of 22/12/1944.

Chapter 5

1. Schneider, W., op. cit. p. 216.
2. Reynolds, M., *Men of Steel, I. SS-Pz-Korps*, Staplehurst, 2005, p. 157.
3. Gavin, J., op. cit., pp. 238-9.
4. Rubel, G. K., 'History of the 740th Tank Battalion' in *Daredevil Tankers: The Story of the 740th Tank Battalion*, United States Army, 1945, entry for 7 January 1945.
5. Fort Leavenworth, Ike Skelton Library, AAR 740 TB entries from 3-7 January 1945.
6. Criba, Liège, Fonds Cailloux, testimony of Cecil Taylor.
7. Wheaton, First Division Museum, G2 Journal and File, 1st Inf Div (ETO), 7 Jan 45-12 Jan 45, G2 periodic report no. 213.
8. Washington, NARA, AAR 320th IR 35th ID, entry of 9/1/1945.
9. Lefèbvre, L., *La bataille de Bastogne*, Bastogne, 1974, photo booklet.
10. Consulted: Washington, NARA, AAR of the 134th IR and 654th TD and Journal of the 134th IR.
11. Summary of the operations of the 987th FAB written by one of its veterans, Harlan Harner,https://battleofthebulge.org/2014/07/11/987th-fab-in-wwii-harlan-harner/ accessed on 15 July 2022.
12. Fort Leavenworth, Ike Skelton Library, N-12472, Order of Battle US Army WWII ETO, Paris, 25/1/1946, p. 137.
13. Wheaton, First Division Museum, G2 Journal and File, 1st Inf Div (ETO), 13 Jan 45-18 Jan 45, XVIII Corps G2 Periodic Report N°28.
14. Schneider Vol II p. 216.
15. Dupuy, T., *Hitler's Last Gamble*, Shrewsbury, 1995, p. 346.

16. Wheaton, First Division Museum, G2 Journal and File, 1st Inf Div (ETO), 7 Jan 45-12 Jan 45, report HQ 5th AD.
17. Wheaton, First Division Museum, G2 Journal and File, 1st Inf Div (ETO), 7 Jan 45-12 Jan 45, V Corps G2 periodic report no 218, entry of 11 January 1945.
18. Wheaton, First Division Museum, G2 Journal and File, 1st Inf Div (ETO), 13 Jan 45-18 Jan 45, 1st ID G2 Periodic Report N°209.
19. Wheaton, First Division Museum, G2 Journal and File, 1st Inf Div (ETO), 7 Jan 45-12 Jan 45, G2 Journal, prisoner interrogation report, entry of 13 January 1945.
20. Wheaton, First Division Museum, G2 Journal and File, 1st Inf Div (ETO), 7 Jan 45-12 Jan 45, 30th ID G2 Periodic Report, entry of 10 January 1945.
21. Wheaton, First Division Museum, G2 Journal and File, 1st Inf Div (ETO), 7 Jan 45-12 Jan 45, periodic report no 23.
22. Wheaton, First Division Museum, G2 Journal and File, 1st Inf Div (ETO), 7 Jan 45-12 Jan 45, G2 periodic report no 206.
23. Wheaton, First Division Museum, G2 Journal and File, 1st Inf Div (ETO), 7 Jan 45-12 Jan 45, S2 Bulletin No 209, HQ V Artillery Corps.
24. Wheaton, First Division Museum, G2 Journal and File, 1st Inf Div (ETO), 7 Jan 45-12 Jan 45, HQ 30th ID, intelligence annex no 1, entry of 12 January 1945.
25. Wheaton, First Division Museum, G2 Journal and File, 1st Inf Div (ETO), 13 Jan 45-18 Jan 45, 30th ID G2 Periodic Report N°212.
26. Wheaton, First Division Museum, G3 Journal and File, 1st Inf Div, European Campaign, 1 Jan 45-31 Jan 45, G3 Journal, entries from 16 January 1945.
27. Wheaton, First Division Museum, G2 Journal and File, 1st Inf Div (ETO), 13 Jan 45-18 Jan 45, 1st ID G2 Journal, entry from 16 January 1945.

Conclusion

1. Point.
2. Washington, NARA, Ethint 10, pp. 24-5.
3. Canadian, National Library, RG24-G-3-1-a, Volume number: 20433, File number: 981.013 (D45), Report by Reichminister Speer on Visit to Western Front, 15-31 Dec 1944 (Translated by Air Ministry, 10 Apr 1948).
4. Including the 202 and 203, which were lost on leaving Tondorf and reported by Wendt.
5. Schneider, W., op. cit., p. 216.

Bibliography

Primary Sources Presented by Type and Order of Appearance

Testimonials

Diekirch, National Museum of Military History, testimony of Diether Kuhlman (6. Komp/II/SS Pz-Rgt 1).

Coffer, L., *The Bridge at Stavelot*, www.Criba.be.

Interview by Christian Dujardin with Mr Jacques Crahay, May 2014.

Testimony collected by Christian Dujardin from Mr Gérard Grégoire, May 2014.

Criba, Liège, Fonds Cailloux, testimony of Cecil Taylor.

Testimony of First Lieutenant Joseph A Couri, quoted in the *Official Bulletin of the International Research Center for the Battle of the Bulge*, No. 3, 1992, pp. 16-20.

Interview with Werner Wendt by George Wendt in 1991, quoted in the *Official Bulletin of the International Research Center for the Battle of the Bulge*, No. 3, 2003, pp.6-9.

Combat Reports

Washington, NARA, no date of entry, S3 journal history, 743rd Tank Battalion 1 Nov–31 Dec.

Washington, NARA, AAR 1 -31 December, 823rd Tank Destroyer Battalion.

Fort Leavenworth, Ike Skelton Library, 30th ID G4 report.

Fort Leavenworth, Ike Skelton Library, 30th ID Artillery report.

Washington, NARA, T78 roll 314, *Tagesmeldung OB West.*

Washington, Library of Congress, GUIDES TO GERMAN RECORDS MICROFILMED AT ALEXANDRIA, VA No. 75. Records of the Waffen-SS, Part I.

Washington, NARA, RG 242 T78 R719, Part 1. Meldung 1/1/1944 schwere SS-Panzer-Abteilung 101.

Washington, NARA, no date of entry, 117th unit journal December 1944.

Fort Leavenworth, Ike Skelton Library, AAR 740 TB entries from 3-7 January 1945.

Washington, NARA, AAR 320th IR 35th ID.

Washington, NARA, AAR 654th TD.

Canadian, National Library, RG24-G-3-1-a, Volume number: 20433, File number: 981.013 (D45), Report by Reichminister Speer on Visit to Western Front, 15-31 Dec 1944 (Translated by Air Ministry, 10 Apr 1948).

Wheaton, First Division Museum, G2 and G3 Papers, January 1945.

Post-conflict Interviews

Washington, NARA, ETHINT 10.

Washington, NARA. Atrocity Trial Testimony Lt Col Peiper. Chapter IV.

Freiburg, Bundes Archives, MSA 926.

Washington, NARA, MSA 877.

Works by Eye-witness US military Personnel

History of the 740th Tank battalion by RUBEL, G. K., *Daredevil Tankers: The Story of the 740th Tank Battalion*, United States Army, 1945.

Vintage Maps

G.S.G.S. 4040 W.O. 1938 Second Edition, 1943 80 Aywaille.

G.S.G.S. 4040 W.O. 1938 Second Edition, 1943 81 Malmedy.

Staff map Stavelot 1903 edition.

Books

Agte, P., *Michael Wittmann and the Waffen SS Tigers Commanders of the Leibstandarte in WW II, Vol II.* Mecanicsburg, 2006.

Bouwmester H., *Beginning of the End: the Leadership of SS-Onbersturmbannführer Jochen Peiper*, Fort Leavenworth, Kansas, 2004.

Cuppens, G., *Massacre à Malmedy? Ardennes: 17 Decembre 1944*, Bayeux, 1989.

Dupuy, T., *Hitler's Last Gamble*, Shrewsbury, 1995.

Fontaine, S., *Stoumont Cheneux La Gleize December 1944*, no place, no date.

Gavin, J., *On to Berlin,* New York, 1978.

Gudgin, P., *The Tiger Tanks*, London, 1991.

Grégoire, G., *Les Panzer de Peiper face à l'US Army,* Stavelot, 1986.

Jentz, T., *The Complete Guide to the Creation & Combat Employment of German's Tank Force, 1933-1942.* Atglen, Pennsylvania, 1996.

Kleine, E. and Kühn, V., *Tiger: the History of a Legendary Weapon 1942-45*, Manitoba, 1989.

Laby, H., *Ardennes 44 Stavelot*, Faimes, 1999.

Lefèbvre, L., *La bataille de Bastogne,* Bastogne, 1974.

Reynolds, M., *Men of Steel, I. SS-Pz-Korps*, Staplehurst, 2005.

Robinwon, W. and Hamilton, N., *Move Out, Verify: the Combat Story of the 743rd Tank Battalion*, United States Army.

Schneider, W., *Tigers in Combat, Vol. II*, Mechanicsburg, 1998.

Speer, L., *110th AAA Driving Hitler's Crawlin' Coffin*, Bloomington, 2006.

Tiemann, R., *The Leibstandarte*, Vol. IV/2, Winnipeg, 1998.

Wijers H., *Die Ardennen-Offensive: Die Brücken von Stavelot und Trois-Ponts, Das Schicksal des Kampfgruppe Peiper,* no place, no date.

Wilbeck W., *Sledgehammers, Strengths and Flaws of Tiger Battalions in World War II*, Bedford, Pennsylvania, 2004.

Wilson, A., *Leap Off: 404th Fighter Group Combat History*, no place, no date.